THE WRITER OBSERVED

HARVEY BREIT

The Writer Observed

THE WORLD PUBLISHING COMPANY

CLEVELAND AND NEW YORK

Library of Congress Catalog Card Number: 56-5311

FIRST EDITION

HC1255

To Luke who talked

To Miranda who listened

60   卌

CONTENTS

CONTENTS

The Writer Observed

INTRODUCTION

DURING a period of about four years, my job on the editorial staff of *The New York Times Book Review* gave precedence for a day or two days of each week to writing an interview with an author. The assignment as a regular thing came about in an unpremeditated way. In 1948—was it as long ago as that?—rumor held that Mr. T. S. Eliot was going to be given the Nobel Prize for Literature. The press, with a strong Scandinavian sector in the vanguard, was intermittently camped in the vicinity of Mr. Eliot's known haunts at the time—the Institute in Princeton, a friend's house in Princeton, a friend's apartment in New York, a relative's home in Boston. But Old Possum had apparently covered his tracks.

At the height of the Nobel Prize speculation—and it was *not* shaking the foundations of *The New York Times*—I met Lester Markel, editor of the Sunday edition of *The Times*. Quite casually we agreed that the prize was Mr. Eliot's, and next I heard myself saying, "I can get an interview with him if you want me to." I felt no uneasiness when he told me to go ahead. I did go ahead, Mr. Eliot assented (I had left a message with his secretary at the Institute and Mr. Eliot telephoned back that night), and though it wasn't an earth-shaking interview, I think it was amusing; and it was after all the only one he gave out at the time. Subsequently, the Sunday editor suggested, in the commanding way he has (or commanded, in the suggestive way he has) that I do what later came to be known as "Talks With——" on a regular weekly basis.

During the period in which I conducted these Talks, I was guided in my choice of "subject" by three considerations (though there were exceptions): either (1) the writer was, simply, very good (Dylan Thomas); or (2) the writer, though not really a writer, was in the news (David Lilienthal); or (3) the writer had extraordinary popular appeal (Frank Yerby).

For this book the second category has been ruled out altogether, and I hope it was mainly this category that Ernest Hemingway had in mind when he remarked in a letter, "What you do is okay, but some of the people you talk to stink up the joint."

When I was first asked to do this book I was filled with misgivings. But then I thought about it over a long period of time; and forgot about it for an equally long period of time; and thought about it again. Some of the musings, considerations and conclusions, direct and oblique, some of which led me to change my mind, follow.

2

To establish an inflexible line of separation between two things has always seemed to me to be either difficult or oversimple. Ever since I read it fifteen years ago, I carried around with me Whitehead's observation, "How an entity becomes constitutes its being." In an unsophisticated and exaggerated fashion, no doubt, it was for me contemporary magic against the static view.

Because of my resistance to an oversimplified order, some of my most pleasurable experiences have come from attempts people have made to define things without slurring over the complexity of the things to come under their sway. I have in mind, for example, the way in which Freud searched for the unimpeachable factor in making a satisfactory distinction between the sexes; or Eliot's rejection, in his preface to St. John Perse's *Anabasis,* of all the apparent distinctions between poetry and prose.

Though there are distinctions to be made between serious journalism and creative writing, I am no longer sure what the fundamental distinctions are. I am sure, however, that the differences between them are not so fundamental as has generally been supposed. The Talks that follow were originally written for a newspaper; now, with no alterations, they have become the contents of a book. And though one may ask the quickest question, that question most nearly ready to be blurted out— "Are they all *that* good?"—I do not believe it is the most appropriate one.

I hope, of course, they *are* all that good. I hope that in a modest way—they cannot be more than modest—all or some of the pieces that follow inform, illuminate, reveal a fresh note about a person or suggest a fresh aspect of an idea; above all, I hope they give pleasure. And they may; and if they do, it will be mainly because the talk is generally honest and what is talked about is of interest. All this—though it is relevant in the showdown between writer and reader—is irrelevant to what I am discussing.

The point is, simply, that the question, "Are they good enough?" ought not to be asked in this context because it is based on a fallacious distinction between journalism and creative writing. The day has passed when one takes a book for literature and journalism for its deplorable opposite: enough bad writing has gone into enough books, and enough good writing has gone into enough journalism to put an end to all such *a priori* judgment.

Whatever it is and such as it is, it seems to me that creative writing can be found anywhere—in a philosophic treatise, a scientific tract, a comic strip, or even in some of these Talks, in spite of their obviously limited ends. Obviously, the end of the Talks was talk. But it had as its complementary end a bit of a portrait. What the "subjects" said, whether in innocence or guile, reflected something of what they were. Sometimes an entire character, life-size, flashed across the medium of words; sometimes a quixotic fragment would peer out from behind the obstructing professional (and I would invariably be reminded of Cyril Connolly's "there is always a thin man residing inside the fat man"); and sometimes there was nothing. The dialectic from week to week was furious and unpredictable.

Of course, I was involved, and many times I failed in my role as catalyst. Some times, though, I didn't have to be one at all. And at still other times, I turned out too hellishly a good one. In those latter instances, so much was revealed that had no business getting revealed that I became overprotective and ultimately failed: the written Talk resembled nothing so much as indeterminate pudding. Through it all I had one main job: to give a glimpse of coherent character *through the talk* and, wherever possible, the act (or gesture).

I don't think I would care to claim a fundamental difference between what I have indicated in this problem and the problem the novelist sets himself. They are in fact quite similar. One, I think, determines character from a multiplicity of correlations, no matter what contrary theory the novelist may hold. (Balzac accounts in just this way for the evolution within the novel of Stendhal's Mosca.) The novelist, of course, may reject the deductive method, but, I am sure, at his own peril and at the risk of losing the true portrait. One may get an *idea* for a character and, working inductively, arrive at the proper corporeal gestures. They are invariably never more profound than intelligent simulations, never more moving than clever illustrations. At the very best, a *Lafcadio's Adventures* gets written, and though it is the most provocative of Gide's novels, Gide himself never became more than a provocative novelist. Is this too harsh? I don't think so. At any rate, we continue to use "lifelike" as a term of praise; it is something of what Frank O'Connor means when he says he likes a story (or character) to be able to get up and walk away.

The differences in what is referred to (for want of a more precise term) as the "creative process" I find just as elusive. Some of the Talks, for example, were written at a heedlessly rapid clip; somehow the process of reporting accurately what had been said was as smooth as a sound carom shot. Other Talks turned out to be a torment: a phrase spoken, and that somehow was wrong, and that yet had to be remedied in order to be just to the whole text. Such Talks took a long time and the interviewer found himself quite thoroughly *engagé*. Obviously, there is no Uniform Law of Duration, or Travail, in creative writing either. Rilke took about ten years to do the *Duino Elegies*; and at the end of them took about the same number of *weeks* to compose the equally detailed, equally beautiful *Sonnets to Orpheus*. I hope I have no need to emphasize that a comparison with Rilke is not intended; I am only saying that some writing can be gotten off without suffering or apparent effort and yet become part of our most serious literature, and that the demands which some aspects of journalism make can be taxing and bewildering.

I found other quite similar problems to those commonly regarded as the property and province of the creative process. Often the right words had to be located (and the search went into the sounds of syllables and the weights of words); and yet had to be accurate just as a word has to be accurate in a poem or story. Even at times the form had to be thought out or "felt" for: one had to know *how* to begin and *where* to end. This form seldom if ever followed the sequence of the oral talk. It was created, whether for good or evil. Disparate parts were juxtaposed. A phrase carelessly buried in the middle was unearthed to make a grand finale.

What an irony! I confess I could not help the mixture of pleasure and shame, of pride and embarrassment, when friends, after reading one of those synthesized endings (and how they would seize on just that!), would remark, "What a perfect exit!"

3

I am a little afraid that, in airing my view of the way in which two kinds of writing resemble each other, I may have in at least one respect fogged the air. If so, I would like to make this the purifier: it has never occurred to me to claim for this book that it is "creative." I was intent only on putting forward what I consider to be a point of a general nature, which was that the line between creative writing and journalistic writing, rather than being fixed and frozen, was broken and fluid; and further, that both kinds of writing did at times present identical problems and that these could be susceptible to similar solutions.

I say "at times" and imply all sorts of qualifications. I know it is a relatively small area of journalism that I am talking about—an area that, by the kinds of ends it holds and the means it uses, is related to the creative process. There is obviously a great deal of journalism that is vicious and, whatever its means are, its end is not that of veracity. Life is too neutral, too complex, too subtle for its practitioners; the events they report and interpret are in the way of their partisan vision and their propaganda aims. This type of journalism can not be included in any of the considerations I have put forward.

There is a still greater segment of journalism that is incompetent beyond the call of duty (beyond, that is, the delimiting tempo and routine of a periodical). The ambassadors of this school are oblivious to the life of the language they use; they are accidental practitioners. Since language is an alien tool, the reality they convey is either monolithic or vague. In this province, Valery's observation that "to write means to construct a machine of language in which the force of the stimulated mind is used in overcoming real obstacles" could only fall on deaf ears.

Both these categories of journalism are drastically remote from literature—the first by its totalitarian practices, the second by its very alienation. There is a third category. Whether consciously or unconsciously, it bases itself on a position directly contrary to the idea that journalism may at points be identified with literature. This category affirms that journalism is hack work; the job demands only a minimum fraction of one's self and effort. In general, this school's casual arrogance is matched by its product, which is casual to the point of being slipshod.

I continue to believe, perhaps naively, perhaps as a wicked rationalization of our corrupting times, that to do a job well means to take pride in what is being done. As we grow older one's revolutionary megalomania is replaced by an infinitely more serious *rationale*, based on a concept of reformism, which gives rise to a belief in the importance of doing things a little better than they have customarily been done. As modest as that. I find myself holding great respect for the creative writer who, for whatever reasons of necessity and satisfaction enters into a less pure medium than his own, yet tries to impart to the standard product some new element, a different approach, the sense of a more intricate dimension.

Because of such reasons, for example, it was with deep respect and less grief that I responded to James Agee's decision to write films—to the further neglect of his novels and poems. It was his decision to make, obviously, and any interference in it would have been both ignorant and presumptuous. The point is, I think, that once Mr. Agee made his decision, one knew he would bring to the writing of scenarios a great deal of himself and his gifts—and both were considerable. Of course, that is what he did. But he would not have chosen to work in a popular medium if he had not thought he could manage something worthwhile, even though he could not minimize the obstacles that stood in the way of making a good film from a good script.

I would suppose an identical rationale is held by as serious a novelist as Budd Schulberg. His excursions into celluloid are made, I think, with complete awareness of the medium's obstructing collectivity, and yet, I am certain, he holds a belief that (with good luck) one *can* manage some serious writing, that one *can* succeed in raising, if only to a small power, the status of the medium. I am willing to suppose that at a minimum there are a dozen or so writers in the labyrinths of the cinema capital that hold similar views and make a serious effort to incorporate their talents into the final product. To my mind, such activity is admirable and constitutes one of the most hopeful signs in a contemporary life.

It is entirely possible to take the argument into a broader area. I do not think it is absurd to view the "twin" or "multiple" or "split" activities of a writer as some sort of safety valve in operation. In *The Sacred Wood*, T. S. Eliot suggested that the creative and critical sensibilities were similar rather than disparate; and further, he felt, if a writer were both a poet and critic, the poetry had less chance of "spilling over" into the prose. It was the mixture that Mr. Eliot found unsatisfactory, and, I think, quite properly: poetic prose and prose ideas elaborated into poetry are not satisfactory. But there was a positive side, too. The point I have in mind is analogous, since the split experiences can operate not only as a safety valve but as a maturing factor as well.

Obviously, certain elements from one field are assimilated into the other, become as it were part of the material. The more elements the merrier—so long, of course, as the "more" is ordered. Coleridge's verse bares its author's metaphysical preoccupations; Tolstoy's fiction is clogged (but never paralyzed) by its author's sociological obsessions; Hemingway's stories spin on an axis of sharply observed experiences. None of these writers, however, suffer from spilling over. Coleridge wrote metaphysics; Tolstoy wrote tracts; Hemingway wrote reportage.

It is fruitful to dwell on Hemingway in this respect. As a short-story writer and novelist, he is closer to the poet than to the reporter. Yet—it is undebatable—he could have made one of the greatest reporters in the history of journalism. The proof is in his fiction: in the blow-by-blow account of a bullfight or prize fight, in a pastoral scene, in a dialogue, in an old man's agony that unfolds with the magnificent leisure of nature itself —it is all exact, meticulous, scrupulous, almost an end in itself. But Hemingway is not a journalist; his reporting is only one ingredient of his art; he is incidentally a great reporter, just as Goya incidentally was.

The safety-valve metaphor is, as I see it, operative in two ways. On the one hand, the novelist who is working for newspaper, magazine or film may be spared the spilling-over; on the other, he may be helped to broaden his art. It is conceivable that many of the talented writers whose medium is the "little" magazine exclusively would find a brief but total immersion into a popular medium more tonic than toxic. It is entirely likely that their novels would gain in breadth and their criticism in power.

I have said it is possible to make this argument with a show of reason; I do not urge it because I realize the question is far more complicated than I have suggested. And there is always the question of which writer. There is always the question of what is good *for* each writer. A few examples will demonstrate just how complicated it is. I was sorry to see Cyril Connolly's *Horizon* go because, it seemed to me, the monthly deadline was an excellent thing for Mr. Connolly and his readers both; his intellectual improvisations were given just the right weight, and the anticipation of the reader was precisely attuned to the quantity and quality. On the other hand, I found myself far more pleased with Edmund Wilson's arrangement to appear in *The New Yorker* at less frequent intervals, only because the weekly deadlines were inadequate to show off Mr. Wilson's prodigious gifts. I am delighted to see critical articles in *The New York Times Book Review* by such eminent critics as Lionel Trilling, W. H. Auden, Mark Schorer and Alfred Kazin because they have taken up the challenge of communicating to a large audience. I am not, on the other hand, delighted to see Faulkner fire his outsize guns into the pages of *Harper's;* I would prefer to see him transpose those ideas into fiction where he is much more at home.

I am distressed particularly by John O'Hara's prose and notions in his role as columnist-journalist. As good a novelist and short-story writer as Mr. O'Hara is, that is how poor a journalist he is. His prose, though appearing casual, is in fact careless; his facts go unchecked; his biases are so rampant that contradictory arguments under his nose are overlooked. By his decisive use of the word "class" to denote his highest praise, Mr. O'Hara is well on his way, if he persists in his course, to become the Toots Shor of Literature. Yet the novelist has the crucial qualities of a first-class journalist: the savage eye, the sure ear, the economical prose. Since Mr. O'Hara does not introduce these gifts into his journalism, one is forced to the conclusion that he does not regard his job as a demanding one. He fits only too well, I fear, the category that considers journalism a hack job, in which the superior man need only be minimally engaged. The real challenges are overlooked, and the rewards are trivial.

To go back, then, to the main point, there they are: the vicious, the inept, the slipshod—they take up a considerable terrain in the map of journalism. None of them can be considered in a discussion of the ways in which the serious side of journalism participates in the challenges and satisfactions intrinsic to literature.

There remains, of course, that side of journalism that does participate, if perhaps only to a limited extent, in the literary experience. This journalism, I would say, is accurate, does justice to a complex reality, achieves cohesiveness without sacrificing the complexity, and creates its own form; through it, by it, the reader is given a living or lifelike experience, as well as the basic, pertinent facts.

Criticism, I think, does not always have to evaluate. To make pronouncements of good and bad, of success or failure, is a subsidiary, perhaps even a luxurious, part of criticism. The main job of criticism is to elucidate a way of seeing and thinking, possibly a way of feeling, out of which sometimes it is possible to make intelligent judgments. As a critic I would place these Talks in that part of journalism I have suggested as having an affinity with literature. But I am unable—and not for reasons of modesty—to make a judgment about them. I do not know that they are good or successful. I am unable to say that I invariably located the salient qualities of the writer I talked to; that when I did (if I did), I succeeded in portraying them; that I often recorded the livelier or liveliest statements; that I always (if at all) found the right words; that the beginnings of the interviews were inviting and the endings complete; that I was bright when I should have been, quiet when I should have been, or whatever.

It would probably be truer, alas, to say that too often I was too becalmed, too often not persistent or tenacious enough, too often, in spite of myself, too altogether horribly obtrusive. The certainties I have about these Talks are few. One certainty I have is that what confronted me in these Talks was not different, except in degree, to what confronted me on other occasions (by other voices in other rooms), when I was writing out of my own need and my own choosing.

And one other certainty: during a period of four years I wrote over 125 Talks. I began to get tired shortly before my third year was up, and I think I requested a halt when my fatigue began to turn into something akin to horror at the prospect of another interview. I know nevertheless that I tried to be scrupulous and to achieve veracity. To at least this extent I appear to have succeeded: not a single writer complained of inaccuracy, not to my knowledge or to the official knowledge of the newspaper they appeared in.

You may well say, " 'Tis a pitiable thing." It reminds me only too much, in a queer way, of Melville's tears when he was commended for never being one day late to work. How fantastic and preposterous! Still, it is all the certainty I have—as well it may have been Melville's—and the rest rides on a million rolls of the dice.

4

To be accurate, to be scrupulous, and yet to admit to manipulations in the published interviews such as those I have admitted to—how can they be reconciled? Words that were uttered by the subject were ultimately omitted, words never uttered were subsequently introduced, thoughts separated in time were made contiguous in space, and so on. All this is true.

But I do not see a contradiction; I would justify it by need. Certain changes had to be made, for precisely the reasons that changes have to be made when one is engaged in transposing a novel into a play, a book into a movie, a musical score into sound.

For different reasons, what may be interesting orally can appear dull when it is spelled out. But if you, as interviewer, were absorbed by the *tête à tête,* do you not, as writer, have to convey that absorption—and not merely by *stating* that you were absorbed? If you were to say you were absorbed at the same time that you had your author rambling on in dull fashion, you would not only bore, you would unforgivably mystify, the reader. To the degree that the author was interesting at the interview, the interviewer is obligated to find written equivalents of what was said, in order to approximate that quality.

It is particularly fair if one considers the *physical* limits of the Talks: meetings seldom lasted longer than a luncheon (those were the longest periods) and the written interviews had usually to stay within two columns (about 850 words).

By the very nature of the circumstances, these Talks had to be essences of talk, sketches, shorthand notes that partially revealed what was potentially a full message. Manipulation was not only consonant with scrupulousness, it was essential to it. One had to condense and heighten, one had to try to find the figure in the carpet, one had to sacrifice detail to gain impact. In short, a good deal of the job had to be symbolic; to try to be naturalistic in so tight a frame would have meant, I am convinced, to be quite unjust. Obviously, one stayed within the circumference of the talk and put forward precisely the ideas articulated in session. But there was invariably an inflection to

be sought for, an atmosphere to be insinuated, an exit to be sum-
moned (summed up). I don't wish to exaggerate the problem,
but these Talks did not write themselves. In a small, exacting
way, "creative" problems arose, and one had to deal with them.

I am aware that throughout this discussion—it would perhaps be better to call it a monologue—I have slighted the main
thing—which is the good, intelligent, perceptive, serious talk
that the interviewed authors handed me on a platter. What I
have been writing about is the role I played *after* the interview,
when I had to record it. The role I had to play most of the time
during the interview was not nearly so demanding; it was
mainly a negative thing I was called upon to be, something, I
suppose, like a decently constructed acoustic. I did try to come
to the interviews devoid of any preconceived notions. I thought
of Nietzsche's advice, "To allow things to come up to you . . ."
I perhaps carried this sense of myself as an unmarked slate too
far: on occasions I failed even to read the book by the author
about to be interviewed. Was this so wrong?

To my own mind, my reasoning was adequate: I was not
engaged in literary criticism; my job was to bring forward the
man behind the book. This engaging rationalization boomer-
anged only once that I remember, during an interview with
Ethel Waters, at the time of the publication of her autobiography,
His Eye Is on the Sparrow. Miss Waters' talk was essentially
religious, quite sweet and Christian, until she learned I had not
yet read her book. I felt the leap of anger in her, and I saw her
grow a little cold, but she was magnificently restrained, until I
unwittingly asked her if she was ever going to sing those
lovely songs again from *Cabin in the Sky*. "Young man," she
said succinctly, "you go ahead and read that book and you
won't ask me such crap."

Miss Waters' beautiful anger, though it gave me pause, did
not succeed in chastening me. I continued to read few books

(though, on occasion, I glanced at some) in my belief that the talk should be general and, whenever possible, away from the particular book (which, after all, was to be reviewed that very week, or the week after, or had been reviewed the week before, by a qualified critic).

There now remains, it seems to me, two additional problems to bring to the readers' attention. One is the question of whether to elaborate on some of the Talks that follow, that is, whether to augment the Talks with additional talk that occurred on other occasions. The other point is a general one and should be very brief. It is, as I see it, the question of privacy, of individual privacy. I do not know that I have arrived at any definite thoughts on this question, but I do know I should like to air them.

5

The question that inevitably arose when this book came under careful consideration was whether the Talks should be added to (updated)—fattened and improved on, and yet tampered with. Luckily, the editors at World and Donald Friede in particular were valiant enough—though I think the phrase is gallant enough—to come out for leaving the Talks intact. I say luckily not because I think the pieces couldn't be improved—far from it—but rather because I like history, any kind of even transient history, straight; I like the record not to be messed with. I feel cheated otherwise, just as I felt cheated when I heard the Hammerklavier Sonata played by a full orchestra, even though it was brilliantly done.

And so the decision, I think, was a sound one: let them be just the way they were, a record of talk by over fifty contemporary writers. Yet the point that was finally rejected had certain merit. For example, running down the table of contents, I note that there are two pieces (one and a half pieces, to be exact) about Evelyn Waugh. I recall a dinner party that took place some time after I had interviewed Mr. Waugh. A few of us, including Mr. Waugh resplendent in black tie, were standing around the kitchen sink drinking our drinks when a post-dinner guest arrived by way of the kitchen (which, in a railroad flat, is often the entrance to the apartment). This middle-aged, stocky gentleman, whom none of us knew, bolted between us to the sink, filled a tumbler-full of water, gulped it greedily down, and only then said (after introducing himself —he was a renowned psychoanalyst), "Ah"—in visible relief —"I have just come from another party. They all talked about themselves. It was boring." Mr. Waugh, gazing at the glass in the man's hand, asked, "And *no* water?"

It was witty as the devil and wickedly to the point. I know I have nothing in the interviews as good as that for revealing both Mr. Waugh's way of seeing, his method, really, and his gift for satire. I know the Talk is deficient in the case of Somerset Maugham. The only evening I ever spent with Mr. Maugham also occurred some time after my formal interview with him. Shortly before that evening party for Mr. Maugham, I had attacked him—I think with severity—for his editorial work on what he considered were the world's great novels. Mr. Maugham had cut these masterpieces. Wherever he felt the narrative was held up, whether it was Tolstoy's or Dostoevsky's or Balzac's or Melville's, there Mr. Maugham scissored.

Finding myself in a corner of the room with him on that evening, I was, of course, civil; not only that, I was charmed. Still, my indignation continued to subsist as it were, and I thought at one point I was given the perfect opening to bring it forward. Mr. Maugham had been extolling the virtues of a Shakespearean authority. "He knows Shakespeare better than anyone living today," he said. "The only thing is," he added, "he writes endlessly and boringly." What could be a more splendid opportunity for me? "Why don't you," I asked pointedly, "cut him?" Mr. Maugham looked at me for a quiet moment with eyes that, I imagine, were cool and amused—though I may have read that expression into what could have been the most non-committal pair of eyes in the whole world. "Because," he said, "the fellow isn't dead yet."

I am afraid that nothing in the interview so effectively conveys the fascination of Mr. Maugham, the ambiguity of Mr. Maugham—that combination of innocence and guile—to say nothing of the iron in Mr. Maugham.

There is no doubt that the Talks would gain if one were to go about adding to them in all sorts of ways. I know, for example, that I could add considerable to the Faulkner piece, to the Frost, the Koestler, the Aiken, any number of others. But I am convinced that they would suffer more than they could gain, and they would suffer most of all from disorder and mess.

I run an eye down the table of contents to see whether I can contribute some additional background information to the Talks in order to further clarify them: I find I am not able to: the Talks are all *too clear*, lacking altogether in the right kind of ambiguity. Though there are a number of things that may be of interest. For example, during the first of the two interviews with Mr. Thomas, he dared me (over drinks) to describe him in a diametrically false way (out of his own kind of anarchy), and I (over drinks) took the dare. But the reader will see how (over no-drinks and a sense of responsibility to the reader), I hedged. Or in the Truman Capote interview, I literally *was* worried over my capacity to describe him: he is indeed a unique vision. It was fear, not boldness, that was behind my request for Mr. Capote to describe himself; and, I must say, he accomplished it with enthusiasm and talent.

I can think of many things of that sort, and there were many interesting responses from the subjects themselves after the interviews appeared. There were some that were touching, some that were amusing, and others that were revelatory. But I find it arduous even to think about recapitulating them. I find I can look back, in order to make some attempt to generalize about them. But I cannot look back in order to relive and revivify them. Each time I do, I turn into a pillar of salt.

6

The question of man's inalienable right to be private is fascinating in itself, but it has become even more fascinating in the light of contemporary events. The time has passed when what a man did after his working hours was his own affair. The separation between the public man and the private man has vanished, and I wonder if one would be far wrong to locate the end of that pastoral condition with the full flowering of the Communist International, which is after all international totalitarianism.

It seems to me, though I am no military historian, diabolically appropriate that the distinction between a front and a rear for the first time in warfare was systematically broken down during the Spanish Civil War. Because what began as a struggle between Spaniards ultimately became a struggle between two types of totalitarianism or Fascism—*le rouge et le noir*. Fascism—the red, the black, the grey—does not make distinctions between a front and a rear; nor does it make distinctions between the individual in himself and the individual in the state. It cannot. Its totalitarian view is total. It is logical: one, after all, goes to the source.

"No man is an island"—what Donne saw as moral responsibility, Lenin saw as political salvation. Since certain aspects of totalitarianism are astute and efficient, because based on the keenest instincts for survival, they are contagious. All over the world the distinction between the private man and the public man has broken down. Now, in the free nations, representatives of government need to know what people think privately in the name of public security. Now, in our own country, we have statistics to demonstrate how we secure the national chain by chopping off the weak links known as homosexuality. And, even at a private party, does a State Department official dare to get drunk? It would not surprise me to learn that the F.B.I. holds a fair log on the fifths of bourbon consumed per week by top and middle echelon personnel.

As much as I hate to admit it, I do not think all this invasion of privacy absurd. In a state of innocence, in a pure field, I would think so. Unfortunately, Communism, with its grasp on dialectics, has shown us relationships of which we were quite naive, or which we were perfectly willing to let alone. Since the Soviet Union is based on a theory that it cannot survive in an alien world of capitalism, it is forced—again logically—to remake the world in its own image. Therefore, Russia introduced espionage networks, fifth columns, legal, semi-legal and illegal movements and apparatuses, with the end of remaking each nation. Concomitantly, it discovered how to remake the individual, introducing into his life ideology, propaganda, systematic lying, and, where these failed, persuasions, the extreme of which has come to be known as "brainwashing."

By all this experimentation, both with nations and with individuals, we were made aware of the fragility of nations and individuals. Polands could be absorbed, Finlands brought into line, Czechoslovakias manipulated. And, contrapuntally with it —and with a "necessity" that Bach never dreamed of—Trotskys could be assassinated, Mindzentys made to confess, Gallaghers converted to collaborators and brutes.

With all this exposure of the weak underbelly of nations and the weak underpinnings of man, who can blame the free nations for their anxiety? Anxiety is something quite different from fear, and different from hate. At this juncture, anxiety is, I think, intelligent. Anxiety itself can lead to intelligent actions—though one would hardly think so. It remains for the statesmen to be discerning in this area. One cannot adapt the methods of totalitarianism, but neither can one try to continue to function as though totalitarianism did not threaten us. We are invaded, all of us are invaded, Russians and Americans, Frenchmen and Indo-Chinese. Even if we were to exclude the human carriers, the ideas invade us, and every man is susceptible to subversion.

Everywhere man is beginning to be hunted. In Russia, in Italy, in Germany, in Spain, he was hunted over and over again, and shot. And when states are afraid, there is no room for the private man. Every man must be a public man.

Some of this exposure of the private man has been going on for a long time in literature. But in modern times it has taken on momentum to such a degree—the amount of biography is staggering—that it must be called a modern phenomenon. Not only that. It has taken on a unique angle of vision. It sifts appearances, seeks clues to character, tries out the keys to motivation, cuts out the dog beneath the skin; its end, in short, is not only to understand the man, not only to make the private man public, but to make the private man that was even private to the private man public. Biography today is the art of seeking out the inmost man. In the name of research, under the banner of illuminating a masterpiece, every sort of private fact must be dragged into public view.

I am horrified by this phenomenon, but my horror does not make me right. I do not know, for example, that a national weekly was wrong—though I do think it was misguided—when in its feature-length articles on a famous American novelist, it disclosed that the subject of those articles was partial to alcohol. It was a common knowledge that had been kept private. I knew about it years before. Years ago I had written a small profile of the author, but I did not write that he was partial to alcohol. To my mind, it was his private affair. No doubt, the writer for the national weekly believed that every fact, private and public (and the more private the better public), was part of his legitimate province. But is it true that once a man becomes a public figure everything about him becomes public, too?

I would be more convinced if I believed that knowing X factor about Mr. Z would help me to understand his work better. It seldom does, though. I object to a critic or biographer or historian rereading a work in the light of a newly discovered fact; I don't trust it. If I felt nothing "deaf" in Beethoven's late quartets before I knew about his deafness, I ought not to feel it in the rehearing. If I did not experience the alcohol in Mr. Z's novels, I ought not to experience it in the rereading, after the private fact was made public. The chances are strong that I would, though. It is difficult to resist hindsight, and biographical revelations give one a chance to elaborate some pretty fanciful interpretations.

The danger in biography is just that: it gets in the way of a fair reading. And how can it really help a fair reading? Did Thomas Wolfe drink lots of liquor? I think he did. Did Scott Fitzgerald? I imagine he did. God knows, they wrote very differently from each other. Two writers might grow up loathing their mothers; it would not surprise me if one wrote glowingly about his mother, and the other merely yawned about his. A good novel or poem, a good painting or opera, are autonomous and quite independent of the creator, and one ought not to correlate the product and the producer. I think it to be true even though I am only too aware that a work of art is in some degree autobiography and confession.

As a matter of fact, it may be because of this connection that I worry about reading public works of art through the medium of private facts. One doesn't, for example, have to be given the fact of Gide's homosexuality; it is intrinsic to his novels. One doesn't have to be told that Tolstoy had some sort of guilt sense toward his peasantry, or that Faulkner experienced something similar toward the Negro people; both guilts are externalized in their fiction to a degree that should satisfy anybody. In the light of this discussion, I reject Mr. Z's alcoholic propensity as the province of the profile. I do not see how it helps anyone or anything; it can only satisfy the basest kind of curiosity.

I can only hope the reader will believe that these Talks of mine caused me considerable thought and on occasion misgivings. I will only put forward two arguments that may prove a consistent attitude. The arguments are simply these: I screened and protected my subjects. Quite frequently in the course of the interviews, an extreme statement was made. I did not grab at such remarks with the thought in mind that I was in possession of something spectacular. Whenever these occurred, I asked the subjects if they had intended to say what they said, and if they wanted to have what they said in writing. And sometimes, though not often, I still did not go ahead with it, even after permission was granted; the effect, I reasoned in some cases, was not commensurate with the possible discomfort that may have eventually resulted.

And one other thing. Though I have always felt responsible toward my work, I never permitted it to get mixed with the private thing. I have had letters, for example, from many writers, parts of which could have made very interesting copy.

Even the letter from Hemingway on page 264 is no exception, since it is in reality a substitution for a meeting, and the questions are, after all, the author's own. There are other letters from him that I have not used a single phrase from, and I suspect it is one of the reasons I continue occasionally to hear from him. I have had conversations with authors over the years, fragments of which were extremely usable. I would not make use of any of it. Out of what I like to think of as my own sense of values—and they may not be the best, and I know they are not the highest—I refused, whenever I was conscious of it, to mix up the private and the public thing. And if the Talks that follow suffer from this limitation, I can only hope that the reader will understand and approve.

H. B.

The Meadows
South Dartmouth, Massachusetts, 1955

T. S. ELIOT

THE latest Nobel Prize winner for Literature, Thomas Stearns Eliot, is tall and stooped, attentive, a little remote, and looks like a trapped, graceful bird. Mr. Eliot was appointed a member of the Institute for Advanced Study at Princeton (no connection with the university except a cooperative one), and arrived there on October 1. In his office a blackboard on the wall beside his desk was covered with neat, complex diagrams. The writer asked Mr. Eliot if they were his (the thought occurring that they might be the residue of a visit from his distinguished co-resident, Albert Einstein).

"I should think little of my gratitude if I didn't make use of the blackboard," said Mr. Eliot with a touch of his familiar irony. "I am working on a play, a poetic drama. I am a very inexpert dramatist," explained the author of the expert and successful *Murder in the Cathedral* and *A Family Reunion.* "I think of character and dialogue, and then reconstruct it for design."

Mr. Eliot indicated the blackboard. "The letters of the ordinary alphabet represent characters in the play. The letters of the Greek alphabet represent characters yet to be invented, characters I feel I need. [Mr. Eliot felt he had too few people saying too many things.] A play has to move in and out, and nobody should be away long enough to be forgotten. That's what I'm up to now. Say I have done a first draft, and that I am encouraged. I should think three drafts would get me near the final thing. But that should take me six months—that is, of available time."

He has no working title for his new play. He did have a rather misleading one for *Murder in the Cathedral:* "The Archbishop Murder Case." It raised false expectations among whodunit fans, its author remembered.

Mr. Eliot was asked if he had heard any advance rumors about his getting the Nobel Prize. He had, but he had ignored them. In 1947 whispers of immortality had reached him. "Swedish reporters," he said, "mysteriously turned up and kept hanging about."

When the official cable from the Nobel Prize Committee in Stockholm reached him, he was immensely pleased. There must have been, it was suggested, some ironic satisfaction as well: now, in the Forties, the recipient of the highest formal literary honor; in the Twenties, Mr. Eliot had been almost universally considered decadent, obscure and a passing fashion.

"It amuses me," he said, without amusement.

("Shall I say it just that way—gently?" I asked. "Say it just that way—gently," he agreed, "for I don't wish to ridicule anyone.")

"The process of advancement . . ." Mr. Eliot speculated. "One seems to become a myth, a fabulous creature that doesn't exist. One doesn't feel any different. It isn't that you get bigger to fit the world, the world gets smaller to fit you. You remain exactly the same. Obscurity in writing is confused with novelty. There is, of course, such a thing as obscurity, but a part of that is getting used to it. You look out the window and you see a dragon and you're surprised. You're not surprised when you look out and see a cow. But we don't know much more about cows

than we do about dragons. . . . One never gets to feel more
dignified than one was. One of the pleasures of growing old is
that you don't worry about dignity."

Mr. Eliot feels that André Gide, last year's winner of the
Nobel Prize for Literature, deserved the award. "However
one feels about Gide's content," he said, "for forty years he
has been an immense figure ('figger,' Mr. Eliot says). There
is no question about his style. *Si le grain ne meurt* is a remarkable book. I read Gide as long ago as 1910. He makes
an impression on you. There is good evidence of it in Charles
DuBos, who was a fine writer and a close friend of Gide's and
who fundamentally disagreed with him as much as I do. But
you have to cope with Gide. *Travels in the Congo* is a
wonderful book. So is the Russian book."

A Harvard alumnus and a Princeton resident, Mr. Eliot
did take time out the other Saturday to see the Harvard-Princeton
football game—in which his hosts triumphed by a score of
47–7. "My interests were pretty well divided, considering the
circumstances," remarked Mr. Eliot. "But I would have liked a
more interesting contest. I have passed the stage where a one-
sided victory is desirable.

"Football has certainly developed. I feel about it as I do
about contract bridge—I stopped playing bridge when it stopped
being auction. Football in America has developed to such a point
that I would imagine the players find their studies a relaxation.
It is a more interesting game now, but it is also a more mystifying
one. So much of it is based on deception. If the players are
deceived, well, so must the inexpert spectator be."

Mr. Eliot had less definite ideas about American writers.
"I can't say anything about them because I don't know the
whole picture. I may have read one writer but not another, and
a reading of the one might be necessary for an understanding
of the other. . . . You'd be surprised at how little I know about

current English writers, too. Up at Faber & Faber [the British publishing house with which Mr. Eliot is connected] I don't have to read fiction. And I don't have to read juveniles. Those are the two things I don't have to read. And as I get older I find I can't read novels."

November 21, 1948

ROBERT E. SHERWOOD

❧

"BEWILDERMENT!"—this one word, according to Robert E. Sherwood, sums up his feelings about the response to his book, *Roosevelt and Hopkins.* Sitting at table in a midtown restaurant, an elongated jack-knife of a man, the Pulitzer Prize winner and author of a number of distinguished plays (*The Petrified Forest, There Shall Be No Night,* etc.), elaborated on his astonishment.

"In writing something," Mr. Sherwood said (his speech is slow, considered, punctuated by thoughtful intervals of silence), "I always write with some individual in mind. I think: I am writing this to please Brooks Atkinson; or I am writing that to please F. P. A.; or I am writing this (when I am writing an article) to please Lester Markel, the idea being that if I can please whoever it is I am writing for, presumably I can please a number of other people.

"Working on the Roosevelt book, I remembered the amount of research I had to do when I wrote *Abe Lincoln in Illinois.* And I thought, supposing there's a writer who a hundred years from now wants to write a play about Roosevelt. I was writing the book for that playwright. I had to present," Mr. Sherwood stopped, and then came back to his sentence, "as accurately as possible the extraordinary drama of those lives and of that tremendous period."

Mr. Sherwood, then, wrote his Roosevelt-Hopkins history for someone not yet born. The quick response of the living took him unaware. "I just never dreamt the book would be such an instantaneous best seller. I thought it would get some good reviews and some violently bad ones. I did hope it would be permanent; that was what I hoped for. Well, all of a sudden the reviews poured in, and I was snowed under. They weren't only good; they were magnificent. And when Harper sent me the sales figures, there was, literally, only bewilderment." (According to late reports, more than 75,000 copies of *Roosevelt and Hopkins* have been sold—at $6 per copy.)

Mr. Sherwood was more surprised and pleased than bewildered by the relative absence of the rabid anti-Roosevelt letters he had somehow expected. Of the hundreds of letters he has received, he considers only three to be the frothing-at-the-mouth kind. In general, most of the letter writers expressed gratitude for the sense the book gave them of the heroic time they had lived through.

He was particularly pleased by communiqués that fall into two related categories: those from people who said that previously they had hated Roosevelt, Hopkins and the whole New Deal; and those from people who liked Roosevelt but hated Hopkins. These letters confessed that the book had caused in the writers some stirrings of conversion.

Paradoxically, working on this eventful and momentous book took Mr. Sherwood right out of the world of events and of the moment. "I didn't know what was going on," he said. "I had to project myself back into the year, month and day of the events of the book. I had desperately to ignore what Stalin and Molotov were saying in the newspapers, for it could very well color and reshape my record of those events. It's most difficult," Mr. Sherwood said, "to write about the immediate past."

The way in which Mr. Sherwood overcame the difficulty was by working in sustained concentration for thirty solid months. His apartment, with all the necessary papers and documents coralled there, became his cell.

"Work was inescapable," Mr. Sherwood said. "I couldn't put on my hat and go home—I was home. I'd start to work while I was eating breakfast and work through until midnight, or 1 or 2 in the morning, when I became utterly exhausted. Nobody," Mr. Sherwood said deliberately, "was standing over me with a club, but I got so interested and excited I couldn't let go."

In direct ratio to Mr. Sherwood's increasing involvement, the book, like Alice, grew bigger and bigger. His publisher would ask him how big it was going to be. "Oh, absolutely gigantic," Mr. Sherwood would say, "about 150,000 words." Later they asked again how big it was. "Oh, enormous—200,000 words." And so it went: Harper would put the question, Mr. Sherwood would add 50,000 words.

It was a long haul for Robert Sherwood—thirty months, 500,-000 words, behind that, sixty months in Government service with nobody knows how many words. Mr. Sherwood needed a holiday—and, as a matter of fact, he said, he is in the middle of one right now. It is called "Miss Liberty"—and it's a musical comedy (book: Robert Sherwood; music and lyrics: Irving Berlin; direction: Moss Hart).

"Irving and I were always talking about doing something together," said Mr. Sherwood. "Besides, I had to do it. There are always ideas revolving around and around in my head. Most of them simply fly off their axis and disappear. Sometimes one idea sticks, persists, and you say, 'I'm going to write it.'

Well, all during that thirty months on the book, I wondered what I was going to do next. A play? A novel? But the 'Miss Liberty' idea kept coming up and I knew that that was it."

"Miss Liberty," Mr. Sherwood revealed, does not represent his first fling with a musical. At Harvard, back in 1917, he did the book and lyrics for the Hasty Pudding show. It didn't see the footlights that year. "The entire cast," explained Mr. Sherwood, "including the author, left to join either the Army or Navy." It was put on in 1920. Did Mr. Sherwood remember it? Mr. Sherwood replied, very swiftly: "I could sing you the entire score right now."

"Miss Liberty," Mr. Sherwood acknowledges, hasn't been easy to write either. He says there's no easy way to write, and the easy way is probably wrong anyway. There are difficulties and difficulties, however. On the *Roosevelt and Hopkins*, Mr. Sherwood said the early New Deal part of the book gave him the most difficulty. As a matter of fact, Mr. Sherwood felt terribly bogged down in it.

"For every step forward I took," he said, "it seemed I took ten steps back. And then I met Gunther and told him about it. Gunther informed me that he'd had the same experience and had come to the realization while writing *Inside U. S. A.* that he could spend four years on Rhode Island alone. That was a great moment for me," said Mr. Sherwood. "I kept saying to myself: Get out of Rhode Island, come on, get out of Rhode Island."

February 13, 1949

EVELYN WAUGH

No matter how you look at him, Mr. Evelyn Waugh is a deceptive man: what meets the eye is at variance with what meets the ear. A remark he makes suggests cynicism, or perhaps a satiric humor, but Mr. Waugh's face—bland, pink and cherubic—suggests only innocence. In fact, expression on Mr. Waugh's face is at a minimum—a flicker of amusement, of naughtiness, an infinitesimal hint of wonder. In feature it's a little like a boyish Winston Churchill's. And Mr. Waugh's bowler, cigar and dapper, plump figure extend the resemblance.

In his rooms at one of New York's most solid and fashionable hotels, Mr. Waugh, smoking his cigar and looking mildly amiable, talked about his newly published novel, *Scott-King's Modern Europe*. He spoke of it in a remote, dispassionate way, a little as though the book had been written by a not-too-promising colleague—and Mr. Waugh speaks only when he is spoken to.

INTERLOCUTOR: It's first-rate satire.

MR. WAUGH *(skeptically)*: Really, you liked it? I'm sure there's a good thing hidden away in it somewhere. There's too much insignificant detail though, too much emphasis on fretful detail. For so short a piece, you know.

INTERLOCUTOR: It is, nevertheless, a very funny book.

43

MR. WAUGH (*skeptically*): You thought that, did you? I wrote it three years ago. After I got back from Spain. If I'd rewritten it now I should get into it more of the real horror, less of the fascination of travel.

INTERLOCUTOR: You made a very good thing of the "Ingrid Bergman" girl, you know, the physical culturist.

MR. WAUGH: Yes, that *was* rather good. There's some false things in the piece, though. The underground man now. He's a man of straw. Never met such a man. Completely invented.

INTERLOCUTOR: The discussion about short and long views at the end of the book gave a depth to the satire—it was funny and it was moving.

MR. WAUGH (*skeptically*): Oh, you liked that? I'm sure there's a good theme in it. But I didn't do it. As a matter of fact *Scott-King* was written very quickly. It was a month in the writing. That means about three to four hours a day at my desk and twelve to eighteen hours of thinking about it. You know, you go out for a walk, get a thought, come back, alter a sentence. The thing grows, goes along. About on the average each sentence is written certainly twice. All from longhand of course, no dictating, no typewriting. Just push the words around and change them, you know.

INTERLOCUTOR: George Orwell, in his review in *The New York Times,* said you had been rude to America in *The Loved One,* but that you had been equally rude to Europe in *Scott-King.*

MR. WAUGH: Not equally. People said I was harsh toward America. Not at all. I was harsher toward Europe. I've more despair for Europe than for America. There's much more wrong *there* than here.

Mr. Waugh has a relish for the writings of Max Beerbohm.

"He is it," said Mr. Waugh decisively. He also admires Graham Greene's *The Heart of the Matter* and Elizabeth Bowen's *The Heat of the Day.*

"She's a good writer. So was Virginia Woolf—within her idiosyncrasies—but she was not as inventive as Bowen. Bowen learned a great deal from Woolf, but is a better writer."

D. H. Lawrence was a bad writer. "Philosophically he was rot," Mr. Waugh said, "and as a craftsman he was frightful." With Lawrence thus pushed to the wall, Mr. Waugh proceeded succinctly to abolish that residual talent the defenders of Lawrence claim for him: namely, his creative psychology. "Psychology—there isn't such a thing as psychology. Like the word *slenderizing*. There isn't such a word. The whole thing's a fraud."

American writers? Mr. Waugh thought Thomas Merton (*The Seven-Storey Mountain*) and J. F. Powers (*Prince of Darkness*) good young writers. "Christopher Isherwood is a good, young American writer," Mr. Waugh said. "I think you can put him down among the American writers."

"The best American writer, of course," Mr. Waugh said, "is Erle Stanley Gardner. . . . Do I really wish to say that? By all means."

Just now, Mr. Waugh himself, he says, is on leave. "I'm a very lazy man. My whole life's a vacation, occasionally interrupted by work. Though I suppose I do want to write a novel or two novels about the war, it would be a study of the idea of chivalry."

What he'd like to write, Mr. Waugh confessed, would be a detective story. "Not like Graham Greene, but rather like the story of the Agatha Christie or Erle Stanley Gardner sort, where the clues are given and an actual solution takes place. I admire very much books of pure action."

INTERLOCUTOR: Perhaps that is because your books aren't like that, but rather are quite the opposite?

MR. WAUGH (*slowly, slyly*): Yes, there *is* some thought in them, I imagine.

March 13, 1949

J. P. MARQUAND

~·~

J. P. MARQUAND, the author of the best selling *Point of No Return,* had just returned from Nassau. Tall, in his middle fifties, Mr. Marquand looked fit. He was quite ready, he said, to answer questions. He felt he was an expert at answering questions. Ever since the time—some ten years ago—when he began to give up Mr. Moto and take on the Messrs. Apley and Pulham, he had been answering questions. He had answered all sorts, but rarely those of a literary kind. Mr. Marquand, then, was to talk about literature.

Was Mr. Marquand consciously working at a series of novels that would constitute an entity, a sort of *Comedie humaine?* There was Apley and Pulham, *Wickford Point* and *Point of No Return.*

"I would like, before I'm through," Mr. Marquand replied, "to have a series of novels which would give a picture of a segment of America during the past fifty years. It won't be universal. I'm not as good as Tolstoy. (And even Tolstoy wasn't universal.) I can only write of what I know and have seen. As soon as an author breaks away from what he knows, he may, if he is good, write convincingly, but not truly. No matter how you do it, you do it superficially; there is not the depth of reality."

Mr. Marquand pursued the point. "I was looking over a series I did in 1934—some blockade stories during the Civil War. 'My God,' I said, after I read them, 'is this what I did?' They're pretty good adventure stories, they're well-constructed, they're deft. You couldn't make them better. They're Monsieur Beaucaire, sort of cloak-and-dagger romance. But they don't have what I call truth. How could they have? I've never been a blockade runner and I didn't fight in the Civil War."

Mr. Marquand was thoroughly aware of what sometimes is called "the imaginative leap." "It was Tolstoy, wasn't it," he said, "who wrote that a good writer who saw a street fight should be able to write a battle. I'm frank enough to admit that I'm not good enough to write about the Civil War. [Mr. Marquand was in World War I.] Though I could put up a reasonably credible exhibition. I remember I thought I'd do a story on China after I'd been there. I've been there a couple of times since. I'm very fond of the East, and I think I have the atmosphere of North China down pretty well. But I can't do it. I've never lived there, I've never worked there. I don't have a stake there. That perhaps is the point: you ought to write only about what you have a stake in."

Mr. Marquand, having a "stake" in the reality and truth of his work, considered his newest hero, the assistant vice president of a bank who almost gives up being a banker. "I was endeavoring," he said, "to draw a picture of an average man. He could have said to his wife, 'My dear, I've tossed over the job, and today is the happiest day of my life!' I toyed around with the idea. But it occurred to me that such an act was absolutely unreal. It isn't what the average man would do—even though some of the critics would have liked him to toss it over. The critics, of course, don't have the problem of keeping a character in character."

Mr. Marquand considers himself essentially a New Englander, particularly in his literary tastes. Of all the books of the past, he most likes to read Cotton Mather's *Magnalia Christi Americana*. "It's a wonderful book," Mr. Marquand said. "About all of the wonders of New England. There are the wonderful ceremonies of the Indians in it. There are the wonderful phenomena of nature, wonderful crimes, wonderful examples of witchcraft and the wonderful sermons Mather delivered to the bondswomen before they were hanged because they had smothered their illegitimate children."

Mr. Marquand continued: "An amazing hodgepodge. But it is the basis of my favorite author, Hawthorne. I'm not sure Hawthorne ever read Mather; though he must have. He must have been brought up on it. Books like *The House of the Seven Gables* or *The Scarlet Letter* couldn't have been written otherwise. I'm very fond of Hawthorne."

Mr. Marquand is very fond of the other "New Englanders," those authors who, in retrospect, make up our "Golden Age." "I'm fond of Thoreau," he said, "because he's written about the country I know. I like Emerson because I like Emerson. And of course Melville. (I'm the only Harvard man I know who hasn't attempted to write a book about Melville.) My great aunt was Margaret Fuller. I've been brought up in that tradition. The most amazing thing is that with only that small hinterland to draw on, there could have been such a flowering.

"I suppose," he said, "when you leave the age of Emerson, Thoreau, Hawthorne and Melville, there is a terrible hiatus— except for two mountain peaks: Mark Twain and Henry James. There are hills certainly—Bret Harte and Frank Norris, Owen Wister in *The Virginian* (I used to know Wister: the portrait of the hero is very interesting, but I have my doubts about the book), Willa Cather, and so on. (I know I'm being awfully cavalier about this.) But you don't get anything until after World War I. What developed then is indeed comparable to the work of the great past.

"There was Scott Fitzgerald (who, of course, never wrote as he should've, never fulfilled his promise). Fitzgerald had as much talent as Hawthorne and Melville. There was Sinclair Lewis, the early Dos Passos, the older Theodore Dreiser, Sherwood Anderson and Ernest Hemingway."

(Asked whether he didn't include William Faulkner, Mr. Marquand said, "Yes, I'll throw Faulkner in—but with reluctance.")

"Of course," Mr. Marquand continued, "when you are looking at an age, at an era, one of the great ways of considering it, to my mind, is to look at the second-rate writers. A first-rate writer is universal. He gives you something more than the particulars of the age. But take a writer like Robert W. Chambers. He's an example of what I mean. Read him and you get much more of the times. All the fruitful details of the average people of the age are portrayed by him and writers like him. Like George McCutcheon, Lewis Joseph Vance and Richard Harding Davis. I really love those people."

Mr. Marquand believes that when he is working, he works pretty hard. He minimizes the physical side of writing. "I sit around and think about it," he said. "The more leisure and freedom a writer has to sit around and think about his characters, the better. The physical business of writing"— Mr. Marquand waved his hand deprecatingly—"is secondary to contemplation. I used to write right off. Now I like to know everything in advance. Certainly everything about my characters."

"I find," he said, "when I am writing a novel I'm dealing in a double life. I live in the present with my family at the same time that I live in the past with my characters. It is this," he reasonably explained, "that makes a novelist so eccentric and unpleasant."

Did Mr. Marquand believe, then, that he was "eccentric and unpleasant"?

"Yeah, I certainly do," he replied dryly. And emphatically added: "All writers should be avoided."

April 24, 1949

E. M. FORSTER

WHEN E. M. Forster was here for the first time just two years ago, this reporter jotted down some impressions of the English novelist, along with some of the then current doings of the gentleman from Kings College, Cambridge. "Very British," he put down. "Bony and angular, with hands locked in front of him and swung like a pendulum. Very pale eyes, quizzical and expectant. Altogether looking like a spare, intelligent, ruffled heron."

Well, two years have passed and most of it holds. Mr. Forster still looks like the heron, and, of course, a British heron. He is still as gentle and abstracted as he was, as disarming (still looking at you as though *you* were the author of *A Passage to India*), as perspicacious and charming. What doesn't hold, perhaps, is that Mr. Forster this time is being more sedentary (last time he went down to the bottom of the Grand Canyon on a burro). Mr. Forster himself was first to say so. Asked if he had any plans or projects, he said unequivocally, though a little wearily: "No plans. After all, I'm getting on. I'm seventy, you know." (His publishers, Harcourt, Brace, are planning for him, however: they hope to collect some of the scattered Forster essays and put out a book similar to *Abinger Harvest*.)

The 1949 Mr. Forster has so far avoided the quite strenuous visit of the 1947 Mr. Forster. He has delivered several lectures

—the most brilliant one, "Art for Art's Sake," he gave at the American Academy and National Institute of Arts and Letters. He also went up-State to receive an honorary degree at Hamilton College. ("I have had a long, friendly connection with them.") He plans to go back to England at the end of the month.

Perhaps the most active thing Mr. Forster has done so far— though nothing so strenuous as his descent down a mountain— was to cross over the river to Union City, New Jersey, in order to take in a burlesque show. Mr. Forster's reactions were mixed and, apparently, it was not a waste of time. (It is hard to imagine that anything can be a waste of time to him.) "I liked the comedy," he said, "the knockabout, very much indeed. But the caricature of the ballet that the girls did eluded me. I think they were taking off the Rockettes. It was far too subtle."

In his speech, in which he had created a kind of rallying-cry for the artist by uttering the phrase "Macbeth for Macbeth's sake," Mr. Forster had made an unusual listing. He had said: "The making of something out of words or sounds or paint or clay or marble or steel or film * * *." One wondered whether any world figure today (and one who was seventy years old to boot) would give to the material of film the same potential dignity he gave to words or sounds or paint or clay.

Mr. Forster did indeed. He emphatically liked the medium. "I've seen films I've enjoyed very much. The most recent was a Sartre. The ghosts in it were more solid than real people. Really, it was quite good. I enjoyed *Henry V,* though I didn't enjoy *Hamlet* so much. I didn't like the swirling. Yes, they were much too fidgety with the camera. I didn't see the point. In India the camera never ceases. I saw a big, quite fine historical film in Bombay that was spoiled by the fidgety camera, too. Though I don't see why they shouldn't do lovely work in India. They've a good climate for it; Indians are good actors and have lovely postures."

Mr. Forster would like to see California again. (The nearest he has gotten to it this time is a long-distance telephone conversation with Christopher Isherwood, from Santa Barbara.) California hadn't been monotonous sky and cloud and sun when he had been there last. "I didn't come in for the famous California weather," he said. "There was a lot of fog rolling up from the sea. A bit out one saw little gray islands, like undiscovered worlds—or the beginning of some odd gray world."

When he was questioned about New York, he appeared a little dismayed. "There ought to be a great deal to say about it, but goodness knows what," said Mr. Forster. "Perhaps I ought to have written it for you. . . . I do like being here. It excites me and I don't think it frightens me as it does most people. I haven't seen the alleged remorselessness."

Twenty-two years ago Mr. Forster published a distinguished book of criticism, *Aspects of the Novel*. One wondered whether he now questioned any of the statements in it. "There are some judgments in the book I would revise," he said. "The more I read Joyce the more I am compelled to recognize his genius. I never can appreciate him; I suppose I should never try. But, reading him, I become more humble.

"George Eliot has gone up for me. In the book I emphasized too much her pedestrianism. She is the most civilized of the Victorians. She and Matthew Arnold. In Arnold it's more to do with the prose, perhaps, than with the poetry. He seems to have foreseen the troubles of our time. Of course, if you get someone who sees them from the detachment of another time it is much more helpful. It's that kind of help that people get from the Greeks. Dickinson [Goldsworthy Lowes Dickinson was the subject of a biography by Mr. Forster] got it from the Greeks. I get it from Arnold. I've never got it from the Greeks."

Mr. Forster hasn't read much recent American literature. He likes Katherine Anne Porter, and he says some of Eudora

Welty's stories strike him "as particularly good."   He did like
Willard Motley's *Knock on Any Door*. (Christopher Isherwood
had put him on to it.)

What had Mr. Forster liked in the novel?

"In the middle of all that drunkenness and violence—which
I do not take to—I saw human values and human warmth.

"Do you know him?" Mr. Forster asked. "Is it true that
he's a Negro? How incredible! How very nice! I think it's
rather fine that there's no inkling of it in the book. I'm glad
we've talked about Motley."

June 19, 1949

ARNOLD TOYNBEE

⌄⌄

ARNOLD J. TOYNBEE is an amiable man. But he can be difficult. It was most difficult, for example, to induce him to get
off the subject of history and those current political, economic
and social events that will become history. If the truth be told,
Mr. Toynbee barely swerved. And yet, one must suppose, it is
natural for one of the English-speaking world's most famous
living historians to be history-minded.

Mr. Toynbee is fifty-eight, of medium height, very slight, of
an almost wraithlike appearance in the slightness of figure and
the ashen complexion. But his fine, intellectual head and hearty,
prolonged, pumping handshake quickly dispel the spectral impression. Mr. Toynbee had just finished his stay at the Institute
for Advanced Study at Princeton (where he has been at work
on the last three volumes of *A Study of History*), and was poised
for his return to England.

"My personal belief," Mr. Toynbee said, instantly coming to
grips with our present historic anxiety, "is that I don't expect to
see a third fighting war, but I don't expect easy relations either.
The cold war will be with us for a long time. By a cold war I
mean a kind of competition between ways of life. What I hope
is that, while we avoid a shooting war, we grow to get less
unlike each other. It might get down to quantitative questions."

57

Wouldn't human beings have to undergo some fundamental changes in order to conduct themselves in so civilized a way? "It's happened before, hasn't it?" Mr. Toynbee obviously meant the question as a rhetorical one. "After a century and a half of wars between religions, people settled down, didn't they? Catholics and Protestants came to recognize that they couldn't exterminate each other, that they couldn't go around trying to."

Mr. Toynbee isn't a Pollyanna (a look at his grave scholar's face should get anyone rid of *that* notion), but his concept of "challenges" does, on occasion, give him an optimistic, rather than a pessimistic, viewpoint. "The Russian competition," he said, "might stimulate us to do things faster, might make us more active in putting into practice our ideas at home. Of course," Mr. Toynbee considered, "the great difficulty in Europe is that the nations are too small for the modern world. Even the United States might find herself too small for the world of the future. We shall all have to consider quite seriously a close association, a union of countries with the same way of life. America is founded on that, though, isn't it?"

Was the Atlantic pact, then, a beginning? "The Atlantic pact," said Mr. Toynbee, "whatever else it may be, is the natural result of centuries of cooperation. As far as we believe in our fundamental ideas, we want them to prevail—and by convincing the others, by making our way of life a good one."

There are heartening signs of democracy both here and in Britain, Mr. Toynbee believes. "The more the electorate makes its own decisions, the better," he said. "The British elections and the recent Truman election went against the press. I'm not speaking for Truman and against Dewey. I am not saying which one has a better or worse policy. (Being a guest here, being a foreigner, I am not really in a position to express opinions.) The only question is that of the independence of the electorate. Perhaps we are finding that the problem now is being able to do more than read and write and having a vote. Being able to do more than that—that's rather important, isn't it?"

Did having a sense of history make the historian into a reliable prophet? "The historian," Mr. Toynbee replied, "gets a general notion of what kind of thing might happen and what kind of thing one must do. There are enough instances of Hitler and Mussolini in the past to know that such men must come to grief, but the historian couldn't say because of such a conference, such will happen."

Were there any Americans who were great historians? Mr. Toynbee thought there were. "Parkman and Prescott," he said. "I don't think a great writer is ever superseded. As writers and as general historians Parkman and Prescott survive." Did the historians of today have any sort of advantage over the historians of the past? They did, Mr. Toynbee thought. "Dr. Jung's discoveries have been very fruitful for historians. So many historical movements take place, so to speak, in the unconscious."

Had Mr. Toynbee seen any influence of this sort on contemporary literature? "I'm rather a reader of Turgenev and Tolstoy," he said. "I've a greater taste for Thackeray than for Dickens," he continued, apparently holding fast to the nineteenth century. "I've a great admiration for *Moby Dick*. I've read it more than once. I've read *War and Peace* three times. [Mr. Toynbee reads the book aloud while Mrs. Toynbee darns his socks.] Sometimes it *is* a little bit boring. The history in it? . . . It does go back to Adam, doesn't it? Yes, yes. It *is* amusing, isn't it?"

July 10, 1949

ALBERT SCHWEITZER

ALBERT SCHWEITZER, the seventy-four-year-old Alsatian
philosopher, missionary, doctor, writer and musician, is, first of
all, very large, very bulky, almost cumbersome in physique. His
mustachios are dense and enormous. His head is bold and
granitic, his eyes are, in context, small and of a gentle intelligence. His hands resemble those weighted stones one sees in the
fields (one wonders how the fingers manage the infinite nuances
of a Bach trio-sonata); his wrists are massively square, connected
without grace or curve to the huge hands. But Dr. Schweitzer is
friendly (one had been led to expect an uncommunicative pres-
ence), engaging, jovial even; his talk is forceful and to the
point; his attitude is kindly, simple and sympathetic (one might
say beneficent if the word did not betray a natural gentleness into
an overly pious significance).

In 1913 Dr. Schweitzer bade farewell to Europe (he was
born in Upper Alsace) and departed for Equatorial Africa, a
full-fledged doctor of medicine. Since then he has devoted himself to the two thousand natives in and around Lambarene. And
since then his fame as a "universal" man (like Leonardo, like
Goethe) has spread. How, one wanted to know, had Dr.
Schweitzer managed to employ himself so fully in a mere
twenty-four-hour day?

"My day is a very simple one," said Dr. Schweitzer, who is paying his first visit to the United States. "The bell rings at 6:15. (I don't have any watch. At least, the one I have doesn't run.) Between 6:30 and 7:30 I take my men out to the plantation. There are over a thousand fruit trees. I'm prouder of that plantation than I am of all my books. All kinds of work get done in that hour, on the plantation, on the roads, which we have to repair very often. It's like getting the motor running right. At 7:30 we have coffee. Between 8 and 12 I'm in the hospital. Each day during this time I take twenty men down to the garden where they work under the supervision of one of the nurses."

Asked why he selected a nurse as supervisor, Dr. Schweitzer said he believed the men worked better for a woman. "Call it," he said laughingly, "the chivalrous sentiments of the savage. Though, sometimes," he added, "the sentiment doesn't exist. Once the garden workers didn't like the nurse in charge. She was too severe. They worked for about two weeks, and then they said to her, 'When are you going away?'

"After 12," said Dr. Schweitzer, picking up the routine of his day (and having disposed of lunch), "there is siesta. Everybody ought to lie down—even if there is no sleep. Work recommences at 2 o'clock and continues up to 6:30."

These four and a half hours are split up between the hospital and the plantation, Dr. Schweitzer says. Unless it is imperative, he doesn't go out after his 7 o'clock supper. The mosquitoes—and malaria—are a persistent threat (in spite of DDT). Dr. Schweitzer conducts a small service and tea after supper, and it is during this time that the musician many musical experts consider one of the finest organists in the world gets his chance to play. "Then," Dr. Schweitzer says, "there is nothing. Everyone should go to bed and wait for morning."

Except, of course, Dr. Schweitzer whose sleeping time is a

baffling fact—it's precious little, anyway. When those around him are sleeping, Dr. Schweitzer works—either on business related to the running of his small world, or on his *Philosophy of Civilization* (the third volume, *World-View of Reverence for Life,* is soon to be published).

His book, Dr. Schweitzer says, is concerned with the basic principles of ethics. "One doesn't heedlessly kill," he said, "because of an innate reverence for life." The leopards around Lambarene, for example, raid the plantation to get at the chickens. But Dr. Schweitzer has forbidden the killing of leopards. How then does he solve the leopard problem? Dr. Schweitzer builds his fences well, and, he adds, "among the leopards I have a bad reputation for protecting the chickens."

He gets on even better with little birds. One winged vertebrate, as a matter of fact, took to hovering about Dr. Schweitzer's head pretty nearly every time it saw Dr. Schweitzer, advancing along with him on his trips to and from the various houses on the plantation. This friendship lasted for something under two years. A very flattering experience for most (see André Gide's *Journals* for a similar, if more effortful, incident), but Dr. Schweitzer took it in his seven-league stride as a gentle mystery of nature.

For the past six years, Dr. Schweitzer says, he hasn't read very much—except whatever new literature has been written around Goethe. He has also recently reread all of Goethe. He has read some philosophy, in French and German and English. Most of all, he reads poetry. (Nothing rests him so much as verse, he says.) He copies out those lyrics that move him, and pins them up around the hospital.

Up until six years ago, Dr. Schweitzer says he could say that he had "kept up" with music. Now he has given up trying. "I am closer to the grave than to the cradle," he quotes from a friend. But how did one of the foremost interpreters of Bach's music feel about the music that surrounded him in Africa? "When I hear it at midnight," he said, "during a full moon, I have to go out and ask them to stop. A full moon is dangerous for them. The noise is an infernal one—particularly when near the hospital. It's very interesting music, but I'm too busy. The Africans have a language in some of the songs that is archaic. The modern generation doesn't understand it. They sing songs the words of which they don't understand. The music of Bach is strange to them, too."

No one coming to Africa for the first time can understand it, Dr. Schweitzer says. The mind of Africa—there are many Africas—can't be easily grasped. A book like André Gide's *Travels in the Congo,* Dr. Schweitzer finds beautifully written, but he also feels it fails to get to the heart of the matter. To Paul Du Chaillu's works on Africa (written in the 1860's) he responds enthusiastically. Waving his hand in a benign gesture, and laughing, he said, "I approve all the books."

Dr. Schweitzer says he has great admiration for the local (French) administration in Africa. "In view of the difficulties they do a fine job." Out of an old colonist's respect for the administration, when Dr. Schweitzer goes to call on the Chief of Government he snaps a black ready-made bow-tie around his collar (just before entering the door).

He has equal admiration for the American customs men too. One of his nightmares in the past has been the lengthy and detailed invoices he has had to make out during his shopping tours (mainly medical) in European countries. "The packing and listing," he said, "Ooh-la-la! When I come here, with so many things, all they ask is do I have any gifts. That's all they need to know!"

Dr. Schweitzer plans to leave for Lambarene on July 21. His only public appearance has been at Aspen, Colorado, at the Goethe 200th anniversary, where he delivered a lecture (new) on Goethe, in both German and French. He has been seeing a number of medical men, both practitioners and executives of medical and chemical supply firms. He is looking forward to his next encounter with the customs men, when he expects he will be loaded down with medicines and the newest formulae for fighting leprosy.

July 17, 1949

CHRISTOPHER MORLEY

"Ask Christopher Morley about himself," a friend of Mr. Morley said to this writer, "and he'll tell you about Joseph Conrad." The friend was accurate. Mr. Morley was full of Mr. Conrad—and particularly so, it being the twenty-fifth anniversary of Conrad's death—and it was only through his interlocutor's perseverance that Mr. Morley temporarily became the man who made friends with himself. "Conrad," said Mr. Morley. What about *The Man Who Made Friends With Himself?* his interlocutor asked hastily, referring, of course, to Mr. Morley's latest book.

"Why," asked Mr. Morley (who is approaching his sixtieth year, is bearded, very burly and as intelligent as any thin man), "are so many reviewers of this book so annoyed by the passion for literature that is in it? But, generally speaking, I am astounded by the critics' generosity toward what is a quite difficult book. I have a feeling about it similar to the one Conrad had about *The Shadow Line*—one of Conrad's neglected masterpieces—in which he made an attempt to be disastrously honest with himself and the reader."

Was it disingenuousness that led Mr. Morley back to Conrad? Whatever it was, one was reconciled for the moment. Mr. Morley pointed a solidly emphatic and eloquent finger at a massive

and weather-worn wheel. "That," he said with relish, "comes
off the *Otago,* Conrad's first ship, which Conrad piloted in
1888–1889. Conrad had a feeling about a ship's wheel; he wrote
that it is a 'symbol of man's claim to control his destiny.' (That
line has always stayed in my mind.) It was Alan Villiers who
told me the hulk was still in existence. Conrad himself didn't
know it. W. S. Hall, a friend of mine, visited the hulk at my request—in a ships' graveyard in the River Derwent in Tasmania,
and we had the wheel shipped here. Mr. Hall and I are giving
it to Captain Sir David Bone, shipmaster and last surviving sea-
faring friend of Conrad, who is giving it to the Worshipful
Company of Master Mariners. The Worshipful Company
museum is right in the actual flow of the River Thames. Knowing Conrad's feeling about the Thames, I feel that's where the
wheel should be."

A most excellent sentiment—but what was Mr. Morley up to
at this time? "Just about ready to leave with the wheel," said
Mr. Morley. Yes, indeed, but getting off the wheel, what was
Mr. Morley up to? "Writing a book of poems," said Mr.
Morley, "a two-poet book of poems. Bill Benét and I are doing
it: I am making a selection of his poems and he's doing a selection of mine. All new. We're doing it in honor of the memory
of Wordsworth and Coleridge, the *Lyrical Ballads,* published in
1798. We're a year late, but we thought of it last year. It's
150 years, and twenty-five years."——

Hastily skirting Mr. Conrad, one did not so much as pause to
fling the question: What about poetry, was it Mr. Morley's first
love? "I can't imagine greater joy," he said, "than working on a
poem. There is no sense of compulsion, or reader pressure, because you know hardly anyone will ever notice it. As Don
Marquis said, a poem is like dropping a rose petal into the
Grand Canyon. There is a sense of absolute freedom in writing

verse. Poetry relaxes. Once, in a relaxed moment, I got to thinking what kind of funeral service Bernard Shaw would have. I wrote:

> *What obsequies for dear old Shaw*
> *Who lived outside the canon law?*
> *Let's give him, to be purely Shavian,*
> *All rites including Scandinavian.*

Shaw wrote one of his postcards, saying he liked it and hoped it would be used when the time came."

Mr. Morley considered further the phenomenon of poetry. "It's also important," he said. "I can say this, a purely personal statement, of course—the novelists that most interest me are those who wrote, or tried to write, poetry. Thackeray was an exquisite writer of verse. You will find it even in Dickens—prose that actually rhymed and that people haven't spotted. Hardy, of course, and James Joyce. Stevenson wrote most delicious verse in two languages—both in English and Scottish."

Mr. Morley surely meant the English-speaking novelists? "Yes," Mr. Morley assented, "the formulation would have to be modified in that way. But there's been a regrettable division between verse and prose in American letters. I have a feeling that our poets might have written good novels. Let me say this—and perhaps I'm taking a sort of daring position—that Ogden Nash could write a good novel. I would conclude this from just two lines he wrote:

> *The old men know it*
> *When an old man dies.*

They are a fine two lines; they have the humor and the poignance. After all, the greatest play ever written was poetry, and impossible to produce. I mean Shakespeare's *The Tempest*—it is laid in the greatest and most impossible of stages, inside the human skull."

Mr. Morley, in the meanwhile having abandoned his office for the neighborhood taproom, stared abstractedly at the tiny flickering screen on which cavorted miniature humans dressed in "monkey suits." "Did you know," Mr. Morley said, "that I covered the world series for *The New York Evening Post* in 1920–1924?" Mr. Morley, then, had seen Babe Ruth at the top of his game? "Yes, the Sultan of Swat," ruminated Mr. Morley. "And there was the Cleveland Indians' Wambsganss. We had a fine name for him—King of Consonants."

The screen invoked attention. But Mr. Morley, after a time, resisted such scientific infiltration. "Let me ask *you* questions," said Mr. Morley. "I'm much more interested in asking them than in answering them. I used to interview a lot of people in my newspaper days. That's how I met Conrad."——

Whom *else* had Mr. Morley met? "I had quite a time with John Galsworthy," said Mr. Morley. "I think it was in 1919, his first visit to this country. I wasn't going very good until, in talking about someone, I mentioned the phrase 'he was getting so-and-so's goat.' Galsworthy stared, and said, 'I don't assess that.' I said if A so conducts himself toward B that he causes B to forfeit his equanimity, then A is said to have gotten B's goat. We were all right after that," said Mr. Morley.

Mr. Morley watched DiMaggio hit to left and drive in a run. "I don't follow baseball any more," he said. "I happen to be fascinated by cricket. I went to Haverford, the first school, I guess, to teach it here."

Lord Dunsany, now—there was a man who was supposed to be absolutely hipped on cricket, playing it at night in miniature on his billiard table. "Dunsany," said Mr. Morley. "Do you know his name?" And Mr. Morley answered his own question: "Edward John Moreton Drax Plunkett, Lord Dunsany. I once wrote a poem about it." Would Mr. Morley recite it? Mr. Morley would:

> *To bedward,*
> *Says Edward.*
> *I'm on,*
> *Cries John.*
> *It helps to shorten*
> *The night, quoth Moreton.*
> *First a glass of port to relax,*
> *Says Drax.*
> *And now we've drunk it,*
> *Mumbles Plunkett,*
> *Come on, old zany.*
> *And so all five, with yawns and snorts,*
> *Having partaken their Cinque Ports,*
> *Are merged in bed as Lord Dunsany.*

"Now, as to Conrad," said Mr. Morley, "perhaps I will write you a piece about him."

July 31, 1949

ANGELA THIRKELL

ON ONE of her rare visits to this country (a visit partly connected with the publication of *The Old Bank House,* her newest and sixteenth novel to be published here), Angela Thirkell was asked what she thought of America. She said: "Why, it's like America. It's not a bit like England."

All of Mrs. Thirkell's observations have something of the matter-of-fact and paradoxical flavor of Lewis Carroll's dramatis personae in Wonderland. Moreover, her looks—she is tall, slender, with a fine-line, well-bred air—suggest Tenniel's Alice, but grown up.

Carroll, however, was only in the mind's eye of the beholder. Mrs. Thirkell was focused elsewhere. "The great English authors," she said with a gentlewoman's positiveness, "are Dickens and Thackeray. I suppose," she said with a regretful air, "what it means is that I prefer the nineteenth-century English novel. I am unhappy to say I have a blind spot for the eighteenth century. I have a feeling for Trollope, but it is Dickens I really care about. Every character is real. You meet them, even the most exaggerated of them."

In England recently, as a Fellow of the Royal Society of Literature, Mrs. Thirkell attended a meeting at which a speaker sounded the death knell of the novel as a literary form. This doom Mrs. Thirkell does not find necessarily far-fetched. "I wonder if it isn't coming to its natural end. It's had its wonderful innings. I've done a good deal of looking at publishers' lists," Mrs. Thirkell added, "and I have noticed the relative unimportance of fiction on those lists. The governments may be contributing, too, to the novel's decline and fall. The general tendency of all governments is to help people not to think. The novel flourishing presupposes a certain amount of leisure. We no longer have enough of it."

Mrs. Thirkell reflected. "The novel," she said, "is a very new growth. It is the youngest of the Muses . . . this Muse has no name even." Asked how she reconciles the paradox of the most youthful literary form becoming so rapidly obsolescent, Mrs. Thirkell hazarded an opinion: "I suppose because everything is going on so much faster." And then, even faster than that, she returned to the nineteenth century.

"I hope I shall never stop reading Scott and Austen. Jane Austen is the only writer who never committed a fault in taste. I think we're rather lucky to have the English language. There are so many good novels in English. There are a few good novels in French and a few in German, but the real flowering of the novel was in England."

INTERLOCUTOR: Isn't there one exception?

MRS. THIRKELL: You're not going to say *War and Peace*?

INTERLOCUTOR: Yes, I am. But I mean the whole great nineteenth-century Russian novel—Pushkin, Gogol, Tolstoy, Turgenev, Dostoevsky.

MRS. THIRKELL: Oh, Russian novels are *so* dull! They make me squint!

With a delicate sigh, Mrs. Thirkell confessed her true sentiments. "I do like novels that make me laugh," she said. "Dickens, bless his heart, does." In the hunt for other authors who might fill Mrs. Thirkell's bill, Laurence Sterne was offered as a possibility. "Sterne?" Mrs. Thirkell paused to think. "Not a guffaw, certainly . . . a smile inside one's self? . . . it isn't what I mean. *Tristram Shandy* is the most brilliant piece of impertinence ever perpetrated."

The universe that Mrs. Thirkell has asked her readers to accept (for the past fourteen of her novels, beginning with *Summer Half,* in 1938) has been Barsetshire, where Trollope was before her. "I don't know how it began," Mrs. Thirkell commented on what became the fixed setting of her work. "It began to come in about my third or fourth novel, and it got the upper hand over me. All my people live in Barchester. What I'm doing is a chronicle of what is happening in Barchester, as the outside world impinges on it. As far as I know, I'll keep right on writing about my Barchesterites."

One book that Mrs. Thirkell wrote was not a novel; it was called *Three Houses,* and Mrs. Thirkell liked talking about it. "It was so long ago," she said, "that I can say it was enchanting. It was a description of three houses that I had lived in. One was a house my grandfather, Burne-Jones, had built [Mrs. Thirkell is also Rudyard Kipling's cousin, twice removed]; another was a house that the novelist, Samuel Richardson, had lived in; and the last was a James II house in Kensington Square. It is a small, good book."

Was it true—one had heard rumors to the effect—that Mrs. Thirkell was doing book reviewing and literary criticism in England? "No," Mrs. Thirkell replied firmly. "I rather agree with William Morris, who said he didn't see why a chap should be paid for writing about what another chap says."

When this chap found himself alone again, he looked Mr. Morris up, and found the following line: "An inherited income gave him freedom to devote his genius as he wished."

August 21, 1949

ROBERT HILLYER

THE occasion for meeting Robert Hillyer the other day sprang not from his recent criticism of Ezra Pound, T. S. Eliot, the Fellows of the Library of Congress in American Letters, & Co., but from the appearance in print of his new book—a long narrative poem—*The Death of Captain Nemo*. Mr. Hillyer—who dislikes a good deal of what is "new" in literature—apparently had suffered no ill effects, no pangs of conscience, from his recent acts of indignance. On the contrary, he looked rosy and fit; he partook of his lunch contentedly ("a mixed salad for lunch, and a mixed salad for literature," he said), serenely one might even say, and gazed about benignly.

Perhaps because some luncheons are solemn things in which the laws of decorum are operative, as if by mutual consent Mr. Hillyer's literary gambits against Eliot, and by indirection Auden (both of whom Mr. Hillyer's interviewer has great admiration for), were skillfully by-passed. But the state of modern literature was, nevertheless, very much in the forefront of Mr. Hillyer's discourse.

"Criticism today," Mr. Hillyer said, "is in a bad, or sad, state. We have no criteria to go on. The critical points of reference are very immediate and therefore have no perspective. I recently read a volume on literature in which there wasn't a single ref-

77

erence before 1900. One would have thought this was not possible."

Had Mr. Hillyer thought about what was to be done? Mr. Hillyer nodded affirmatively. "Today," he said, "we need a new periodical that would establish standards. It would be dogmatic if need be, and polite if need be. And we would need someone like Dr. Johnson to run it." Mr. Hillyer considered an earlier remark of his, apparently deciding to modify it: "As a matter of fact, I think there are criteria, and I think they work. The trouble is most critics haven't enough background to use them."

As in most situations today, one cannot be above the battle; within the world of letters, as Mr. Hillyer sees it, one must take sides, too. "In general terms," he said, "literature seems to be dividing between those of us who hate it and those of us who don't. Contemporary literature belongs to the machine age, to an age that makes war along with machines. . . . How is it visible? I see it in the novel, which today is an art—if it is an art—of desire to pull people down and show them their follies rather than their virtues. It is an art of the justification of the unbalanced and a suspicion of the balanced."

Mr. Hillyer paused, then went on flatly: "Nothing would get done, no ship would sail, no food get grown, if the human race were caught in the mood of these intellectuals."

Mr. Hillyer turned to talk of Robert Bridges, a poet he greatly admires. "I guess," he said, "I'm just about the earliest admirer of Bridges I know. Yeats gave me a copy of Bridges when I was nineteen. Bridges and Yeats are both very chastening. After I met Yeats in New York, he said to me: 'If you don't know Bridges, you don't know English lyric poetry.' Bridges' verses are the nearest perfect lyrics of our time—within their intention, of course."

Mr. Hillyer was unable to recall much about Yeats the man

during Yeats' visit here. He does retain one picture of the great Irish poet. It was the occasion of a fairly large afternoon party and Yeats, apparently fascinated, was going around abstractedly counting the cocktails on his fingers.

Mr. Hillyer says that Bridges was really prepossessing. "A tall, spare man, a very handsome old man, with piercing blue eyes and a white beard, who looked like a Viking in training. He talked entirely about other poets—which was typical of him. He was completely the artist," Mr. Hillyer concluded.

Mr. Hillyer warmed to his concept and the paths it led him on. "People talk about this century being devoid of great poetry," he said. "On the contrary, it is a very rich century. I try to look at literature from the point of view of what I think may be true several hundred years hence—it keeps you from the fads and off the bandwagons."

Who among the modern poets did Mr. Hillyer think would be "true" several hundred years hence? "I would say Bridges," Mr. Hillyer replied, "and Frost, Edward Arlington Robinson, Yeats, Housman, Hardy, Hopkins, Dickinson, the early Millay, Hodgson, de la Mare." Wouldn't Wallace Stevens make it? he was asked. "Stevens might make it with a piece or two," Mr. Hillyer replied amiably.

"Don't forget, though," he said, resuming a stricter course, "this anthology I'm talking about is an anthology of taste, not of literary history. You may not like certain things, and yet they can be important, in the way they influence later peoples. Take *Ulysses*. It may be awfully boring, but it *is* literary history."

August 28, 1949

JOHN O'HARA

As HAS been said before, John O'Hara (whose new book *A Rage to Live* has been stirring up the literary and psychiatric factions) was a jack of all trades and a master of some—being at various times a steel-mill roughneck, a soda-jerk, secretary to Heywood Broun and guard in an amusement park. As well as a pretty fair newspaper man. Now Mr. O'Hara isn't scattering himself about: he's strictly a writer and, as all hands agree (even if they disagree about the new book), a pretty fair one, too.

Mr. O'Hara looks less the writer than the steel-mill rough-neck he once was. That, of course, is in the tradition of American writers who, it seems, just don't like to *look* like writers. He's a big guy with powerful wrists and hands and carries an over-all noncorpulent weight of 205 pounds. He looks as if he could do all right in a brawl either with man or bear. He is also doing all right just as a literary fellow—the Book Find Club has taken *A Rage to Live* as its September choice.

Mr. O'Hara was naturally interested in talking about his controversial new book. "I couldn't have written it," he said, "at the time I did *Appointment in Samarra*. I wrote *Samarra* in '33. But all the while I wanted a hell of a lot to write the other novel, the novel that any guy wants to write who has lived in a town just short of being New York, Los Angeles, Philadelphia or Boston.

"In these towns there is always a family, not necessarily the richest one but the snappiest one, that sets the tone in manners, sure; but also in cars and horses. Say, thirty-five years ago, there would be one snappy family, and they would put their money into a hunter rather than into a Marmon or a Pierce."

Did Mr. O'Hara consider *A Rage to Live* a departure from his earlier work? "Yes," Mr. O'Hara said. "The earlier books were special books about specialized people; but this is the big one, the over-all one."

Mr. O'Hara, having been a newspaper man, undoubtedly was aware of the argument about whether the occupational hazards of the fourth estate had beneficial or disastrous effects on the creative novelist. What, one wanted to know, were Mr. O'Hara's findings? "The newspaper influence," Mr. O'Hara said, "is a good one for the writer. It teaches economy of words. It makes you write faster. When you're on rewrite as I was, you can't fool around at half-past nine trying to write beautiful lacy prose."

Mr. O'Hara wasn't the one, obviously, for a rich or luscious (or lacy) metaphor. "Prose writing in 1949 I don't think should be anything but accurate. I keep away from figures of speech. I can compare my car [a low-slung, fireman's red British toy of a car] with my favorite horse—War Admiral. I love them both and they're little and fast. But the comparison wouldn't go very far because there's no clash of temperament between a four-cylinder English car that I drive as there is between me and a horse I might ride, especially at my current weight."

Mr. O'Hara then quit his vehicular illustration. "It's the workman that I like in literature," he said. "I like John Steinbeck because he works all the time. . . . Who else do I admire? Like everybody else, I'm looking forward to that Hemingway book like a kid waiting for the Fourth of July. I don't think the Pulitzer Prize was ever more deserved than by James Gould Cozzens—and he's one man I don't know. Of course, I admire work when it isn't work per se—when it's good work is what I mean. Faulkner is the genius—the only genius so far as I'm concerned."

Would Mr. O'Hara try to tell why? "This is not the standard thing," he replied. "The reason Faulkner's work is so good is that so much of it stays. I happen to know Faulkner writes practically on the head of a pin; his calligraphy is so small he could write one of his long chapters on a single piece of copy paper."

One wondered whether this interesting biographical fact was relevant. Mr. O'Hara said, smilingly, that perhaps it wasn't. However, it did finally turn out to have a connection with what he meant by Faulkner's genius. "Knowing Faulkner as well and as slightly as I do, it seems to me there is no awkward transition from the brain to the printed page. Whereas some of us lose from the thinking to the ultimate work."

"Did you know," Mr. O'Hara asked, "that one of the reasons you don't get flora in my work is that I'm color-blind? I probably can't identify six flowers. But I can identify everything on a farm (my father had one). I can tell you all the differences between a Guernsey and a Jersey (anybody can tell a Holstein). I can tell by the texture of the milk."

There are more darned things in Mr. O'Hara, this interviewer concluded, than were dreamed of in his philosophy.

September 4, 1949

NELSON ALGREN

⌁

THIS department observed recently—the observation having been driven home during a talk with the author of *A Rage to Live*—that American writers don't *look* like writers. Well, this department has seen it all now and it offers an award—if it had an award—to Nelson Algren for being the writer who least looks like one. Mr. Algren doesn't even *sound* like one. He speaks what is (this interlocutor is convinced) a run-of-the-mill Chicagoese, an unpretentious colloquial. He looks like any guy—medium height, medium slim, medium sandy hair—and could be anything: a clerk, a sailor, a baker's boy, a soda-jerk, an electrician, a bus driver. But not a writer.

Obviously, Mr. Algren *is* a writer—and from what the critics say about his most recent novel, *The Man With the Golden Arm*—a very good one. Mr. Hemingway, Mr. Algren says, once said he was one of the best. This is how the story goes. Hemingway, asked who was America's first writer, unhesitatingly replied Faulkner was, and, when pressed for more names, added Algren's. Mr. Algren disparages the story a bit. "Hemingway says something one time that he won't say another."

He thought further on it. "Naturally," he said, "I was very gratified. I was told, I was told over the phone. To be put in the same company as Faulkner. I don't think there's been anything better written than *A Rose for Emily* unless it's *Fifty Grand*. I think there's nobody better than Faulkner and Hemingway. They're in another league, they're in another league over and above Washington Irving, Henry James or Hawthorne who anyway are the dullest writers that ever walked in shoe leather."

Wasn't perhaps the difference a difference in time? The short story had certainly made great strides recently. "The writers today do have the advantage of time," Mr. Algren said. "They can build on the effort that someone like Hawthorne made, that someone like Hawthorne made, sure—but Faulkner and Hemingway are more gifted even than Melville, to express a prejudice. To express another prejudice, there never was a really gifted short story writer in America until Stephen Crane came along."

Mr. Algren came along to visit while en route to Chicago after having spent four months in Europe and North Africa. In Italy he saw Silone, and in France, Sartre. What about the man Sartre? From what Mr. Algren observed, it turned out, Sartre had been influenced by America in subtle ways that one would not have expected—he, too, doesn't *look* or *sound* like himself.

"My relationship to Sartre," said Mr. Algren, "wasn't literary. I never got a glimmer of what existentialism is. Never in our conversation, never in our conversation did it have any relevance. He never brought it up. He doesn't carry his existentialism around with him at all."

Was Mr. Algren returning to Chicago in order to return to work? Mr. Algren, it turned out, didn't have any plans. "I hope to write another book in time," he said. "Just feel around, just feel around in the dark until I get something tangible. Whatever it will be, it's three or four years away. I work like a tortoise. I took three years to do this new book."

It was something of a relief to run into a writer who didn't turn out a book or three a year. Mr. Algren nodded. "Yeh, there's too much pressure on writers to turn things out. . . . What's the solution? The only solution is to resist so far as you can. The more you can resist the better you'll be. You got to make up your mind to do without money."

Back in Chicago did Mr. Algren know Willard Motley—a writer who had done without money for a long time and who, a few years ago, had hit the jackpot with *Knock on Any Door*?

"Sure. I had a funny thing with him. I was sitting in his place, drinking, and I felt uncomfortable because I knew I was going to bum-rap the book, because I knew I was going to bum-rap his book. I didn't like it. I finally told him I didn't know if it was all right to drink his whisky when I was going to bum-rap his book. Willard said 'sure, drinking my whisky doesn't oblige you to like my book. You can express your disappointment in my work and still drink my whisky.' We're pretty good friends," Mr. Algren concluded. "Only no one sees him much. He's private, has a lot of humility."

Mr. Algren's interviewer came away from Mr. Algren thinking the young man from Chicago—he's just 40—has a good deal of humility too. Mr. Algren wrote his first story in 1933—when he was holed up in an abandoned filling station in Texas. Whit Burnett bought the story for *Story Magazine*. Mr. Algren has never been deflected since—though the war did get hold of him and tried its hardest. How had Mr. Algren made out?

"Well, all I can say," he said, "is that I went in the Army a private, stayed three years, and came out a private. I don't know why I should be proud. I don't know why I should be proud of having failed in a military career. But I do have a sneaking pride."

October 2, 1949

ALAN PATON

~~

THIS reporter saw Alan Paton on the eve of his leaving for England to receive a special literary award from *The London Times* for his distinguished novel, *Cry, the Beloved Country*. In New York he had seen the "musical tragedy" version of his novel; in London he will put the finishing touches to the screen version of it for Alexander Korda.

About the award Mr. Paton said: "The *Times* gives a literary prize for the best and most important book of the year. The prize went to Winston Churchill's *The Gathering Storm*. In any year, any book Mr. Churchill writes—especially given the topic on which he was writing—must be the best and most important book of the year." The *Times*, apparently feeling they'd like to do something for Mr. Paton's novel, created a special prize.

Mr. Paton, in his middle forties, the son of a Presbyterian Scotsman, was born in South Africa, where he grew up and where he did everything (from pedagogy to penology) but write. It was after the war that he got started, and in a far-away country. He held the manuscript for a time after finishing it, it was a private matter, and not for publication. But a friend gave him wise counsel. Now Mr. Paton's life is changed. "I am in a dilemma," he says (pronouncing it *digh*-lemma). The reader, however, need not concern himself with Mr. Paton's dilemma.

Mr. Paton, small and wiry and with a lean and hungry look, is an impressive gentleman. His mind is lucid and tough, his speech is precise, unembellished and neutral, yet nevertheless touched as though with a bitter memory. The over-all sense of him is of iron—iron-minded, iron-willed and iron-muscled. If the impression Mr. Paton inevitably gives is roughly accurate, dilemmas will get resolved in double time.

When he was asked if he would talk about the South African Negro and the American Negro, Mr. Paton nodded affirmatively, thought for a few moments, then spoke in an exact, nearly formal platform manner. "The first great class of Negroes in South Africa one might still call tribal," he said. "Even so, they don't lead a life completely untouched by Europeans. From a tribal life they go to the mines and industry—mainly the mines. They, as a rule, are the most primitive of South Africans.

"You have a second great class, those who live on the white farms in the country. The great tendency, however, is for the most intelligent of them to drift away from the farms and go to the cities and then you get the third great class—already broken from the tribal and rural life and become somewhat urbanized. They are much more in touch with the ideas of the world.

"Already there is emerging a fourth group, also preponderantly urban—teachers, ministers, doctors, business men. Oh, they form what may be called an African intelligentsia. They read books and newspapers. They know a great deal of what is going on in the world. They provide the political leadership. On the whole, they tend to become embittered and to feel frustrated. And already there is a tendency among them to look to themselves for their own salvation and even to scorn cooperation with those white people who have always devoted themselves to the cause of their advancement."

What percentage of the population did the Negro make up? Mr. Paton nodded agreeably. "About 75 per cent," he said, "and it is for that reason that the white man fears his advancement. And it is this fear which is responsible for much of the legislation. I think it should be made clear that our parliament and senate are entirely white.

"The American Negro, for his numbers, has produced a far greater proportion of eminent and distinguished men. The reason for this is, of course, that there are not so many barriers toward his advancement as in South Africa; and the reason for that is, of course, that they constitute a much smaller percentage of the population, and that therefore the white American is less afraid of according him these privileges. At the same time I do not underestimate the great power of the American conscience. I do not suppose for a moment that it is just a matter of statistics. We in South Africa also have a conscience. But our fears are so great that the conscience is not so clearly apparent."

What was Mr. Paton going to do next? "My book," he said, "has had such a terrific backwash that I have not had time to sit down to do more work." What was Mr. Paton going to do about that? (It was here that Mr. Paton faced a certain *digh*-lemma.) "I haven't yet discovered whether I would write more if I went back to affairs, to a life of active participation in society. It just might be that I'm not the sort of person who can withdraw to some secluded spot and write books. I haven't yet found an answer to that question. But my mind is full of ideas and I should like nothing better than to be left alone to work some of them out."

He paused, a barely ironic pause. "However," he continued, "I am now expected to lend support to innumerable causes to which people suppose—and rightly suppose—I'm sympathetic. One cannot withdraw entirely from such participation, and so I still find myself going through an extremely difficult stage of adaptation and adjustment."

What sort of literature, Mr. Paton's interlocutor asked, moved him? "If you asked me," Mr. Paton replied, "what kind of topics appealed to me in writing, I would have to confess to you that I couldn't bring myself to write any book which would increase the amount of depression and dejection that exists in so many people already."

But how would it be known whether a book would depress and deject? There was proof everywhere that depressing material did not need to depress. There was the idea of the catharsis. "Ah, yes," Mr. Paton said, "that's a different thing where writing tragedy brings out a catharsis. My objection isn't to tragedy, because I believe tragedy and human life are inseparable. I believe that human life is meaningful and purposeful, and just to write a story of human corruption—I think I could write it as horribly as anyone [from out the stern face there issued, surprisingly, a brief, loud laugh]. I don't find corruption a fascinating or rich theme to write about.

"I should like to write books about South Africa which would really stab people in the conscience. I don't see any point in writing provocatively for the sake of being provocative, or antagonizingly for the sake of being antagonizing. But I do believe there is a level at which one can write where it is no longer a question of provoking or antagonizing, but simply a question of stating an overwhelming truth that a man just cannot deny. He may still be angry with you for having presented the truth, but he is not angry with you for the way in which you've presented it. After he has confronted the truth in that fashion, he is not the same man again."

Mr. Paton stared sternly at his interviewer. Was it the end, was Mr. Paton finished? No, Mr. Paton was not finished. "One rather good critic," he said, "entitled his review of my book, 'A Gentle Protest.' But I believe the book is not so gentle as it looked. What looks gentle is often far more powerful than all the ranting and raving in the world. And it is my hope to go on touching the conscience of South Africa in this fashion. But I haven't purely a moral purpose. I also believe in the task of trying to interpret South Africa to the South Africans so that they can see themselves without illusions. It is a very fascinating and exciting task."

That, it was suggested, ended the talk rather nicely.

"Let us end it," Mr. Paton said, "while there is an end."

November 20, 1949

ROBERT FROST

THE other day a select literary audience gathered to pay tribute
to America's leading poet, Robert Frost. This reporter saw Mr.
Frost before the ceremonies. He found the seventy-four-year-old
poet in good form—a gracious, alert, somewhat shy man, whose
powerfully sculptured head was made gentle by the softness of
his deep-set eyes. Mr. Frost talked—without colloquialisms or
pretensions—in a slow, engaging and impersonal manner that
somehow created an extraordinary effect of a man's intactness
and incorruptibility.

Someone once said about Rilke that he carried his own atmosphere with him. It was so that morning with Robert Frost, and
this reporter settled into Mr. Frost's enveloping atmosphere of
quiet and contemplation and gentleness with an alarming—and
a very real—alacrity.

There was no universe—to use Mr. Eliot—"to roll up into a
ball to ask an overwhelming question." There were many questions, small ones, perhaps, about poets and poetry. "I don't go
delivering opinions about other poets," said Mr. Frost in his
deep poet's voice. "I have my opinions, of course, opinions that
are the result of a slow growth. There's always tentativeness,
isn't there? It's the same as with the bomb. You don't go around
screaming about it. The next day you may have a new opinion."

What did Mr. Frost have to say to the young poet today? "One thing I care about," Mr. Frost said evenly, "and I wish young people could care about it, is taking poetry as the first form of understanding. Say it: my *favorite* form of understanding. If poetry isn't understanding all, the whole world, then it isn't worth anything. Young poets forget that poetry must include the mind as well as the emotions. Too many poets delude themselves by thinking the mind is dangerous and must be left out. Well, the mind is dangerous and must be left in.

"If a writer were to say he planned a long poem dealing with Darwin and evolution, we would be tempted to say it's going to be terrible. And yet you remember Lucretius. He admired Epicurus as I admired, let's say, Darwin. And he wrote a great poem. It's in and out, sometimes it's poetry, sometimes intelligent doggerel, sometimes quaint. But a great poem. Yes, the poet can use the mind—in fear and trembling. But he must use it."

Mr. Frost mused aloud. "A fellow once said to me the trouble with you is that you write on subjects. I replied, the trouble with you is that you write on small bric-a-brac. I am not a regionalist. I am a realist. I write about realms of democracy and realms of the spirit. The land is always in my bones. Someone once asked me if I was for democracy or against it and I could only say that I am so much of it that I didn't know. I have a touchiness about the subject of democracy, of America. It amounts to a touchiness. I know how much difficulty there is about democracy, and how much fun it is, too."

Of all modern poets, perhaps only Yeats and Frost had managed in their best work a simplicity out of complexity—which led Mr. Frost's reporter to the question of obscurity in modern verse. "You know," Mr. Frost said, "if the obscurity was really a new thought, if it was really that—but if it was a slackness, a not thinking through and getting to the right phrase, I couldn't be bothered with it. The test is when you've worried a poem out. Then you should know whether you've got anything really new —we won't say original, but we can say a fresh thought. For instance, follow what you get out of a man like Matthew Arnold, who was confident and authoritative in his prose and a lost soul in his poetry. You get that lostness in phrase after phrase in his poetry. (It's by phrases that you know a man.) Arnold has explained the academic world to me."

Mr. Frost leaned back and declaimed: " 'A plain where ignorant armies clash by night.' There is in the line the idea that the world is meaningless, is corrupt and impure. Arnold says—I don't remember exactly—'Let the long contention cease, Geese are swans and swans are geese.' It's the despair from sitting out instead of sitting in. Arnold is asking too much. We all who are literary feel a little of that. But there is difference and harshness and difficulty and that's all right. You have to be blinded by something. There has to be a blinding light. Love has to be blinding to make things right."

Mr. Frost's visitor recalled an aphorism of Pascal: "The heart has reasons which the reason knows not of." Mr. Frost nodded. "Yes," he said, "Pascal's is a great kind of mind that has to be in poetry. If those things that Pascal knew are not in poetry, then you're just fastidiating along, wantoning along."

What about the gold medal? What was it for? "The gold medal," Mr. Frost said with both amusement and defiance, "means all of me, my *Complete Poems*. Six hundred pages written in the last sixty years. That's all of me."

November 27, 1949

WILLIAM CARLOS WILLIAMS

THE following judgment is made in all honesty and with due consideration: the sixty-six-year-old poet and pediatrician, William Carlos Williams, has more intellectual *vitality* than any poet or two pediatricians this side of the Atlantic. Dr. Williams, tall and bony, with graying hair, and whose bold features have been softened a little by his labors with humans as well as with the humanities, speaks with spectacular vigor on subjects ranging from art to zoology, in a voice that subtly twangs with cosmic impatience.

This reporter recalls with deep fondness the too infrequent visits he made to Rutherford, New Jersey (where Dr. Williams was born and lived and continues to practice medicine), when he would accompany the doctor—in a fading jalopy—on his rounds. The poet would leave his car, usually quite in the middle of discussing a complex idea, to attend an expectant mother; and the doctor would return fifteen minutes later to pick up the idea without the loss of a syllable. It was something better than memory: it was proof—if it ever was needed—of Dr. Williams' profound interest in ideas.

The other week Dr. Williams' third volume of a four-volume poem he calls *Paterson* was published. In a few weeks, New Directions is to bring out a critical study of both Dr. Williams' poetry and prose. Is no man a prophet in his own country? In truth, Dr. Williams is better known in the foreign capitals. But many young American poets know Dr. Williams and are indebted to him—both for his sincere and continuous encouragement and his honest and constructive criticism of their work.

Pound was always in the news and Dr. Williams was an old friend. This writer remembered an amusing story that ultimately Dr. Williams remembered. "When I was at the University of Pennsylvania, around 1905, I used to argue with Pound. I'd say 'bread' and he'd say 'caviar.' It was a sort of simplification of our positions. Once, in 1912 I think it was, in a letter (we were still carrying on our argument) he wrote, 'all right, bread.' But I guess he went back to caviar."

Asked about the state of verse today, Dr. Williams pitched in, with apologies to nobody. "Poetry is in a chaotic stage," he said. "We have to reject the standard forms of English verse and put ourselves into chaos on purpose, in order to rediscover new constellations of the elements of verse in our time. We have to break down poetry into its elements just as the chemists and physicists are doing. In order to realize ourselves. In order to reform the elements."

Dr. Williams' shrug was one—if it is possible to imagine it —of combined friendliness and anger. "The possibilities are infinite in our day. I don't believe about talk in the future. We are not men if we presume that the old boys were men and we're to go ahead and copy them. We then become mere replicas of the past and don't exist in our own right. It wouldn't be difficult for Braque to paint a Titian. But what would it be? Whereas, if Titian existed today he wouldn't be like Titian. He'd show us how to paint. Let's forget about the burden, the thought the poem might carry; and let's recognize the mechanism that can carry the sense, any sense. Think of Gertrude Stein: to use words as objects out of which you manufacture a little mechanism you call a poem which has to deliver the goods. That's what poetry must be.

"I think we're succeeding to some extent in expressing what is in our own day." He was too absorbed—or too indifferent— to notice that he was very close to heresy. "There is a much more intelligent interest in modern poetry now. It's been true for the last ten years. Probably it's the young instructors in the colleges. To say we're becoming crude is insane. Our poetry, our mechanisms, are much more delicate today. We're much more alert to life after a Freud and a Whitehead."

To ask an old friend (and youthful poet) like Dr. Williams *the* question was embarrassing. And yet it had to be asked. Dr. Williams was, of course, unembarrassed. "Why do we have to be so obscure?" he asked. "Obscurity," he answered, "once it is penetrated, is found to be a relatively simple matter. Obscurity is a very necessary impact to the listener and reader when anything really new is presented. The mind is conditioned to the past. Once a man has penetrated the obscure jungle he is likely to come out on the plateau where he has a much broader vision than he ever knew in the past.

"When you think of Wagner (how he was damned!) and Ibsen, and, of course, many others! The term esoteric," Dr. Williams concluded with amused irony, "was first applied to Aristotle."

January 15, 1950

HENRY GREEN

THERE was nobody named Henry Green registered at the hotel where Henry Green was staying. This was as it should be. Henry Green being a pseudonym, it was something of a justice that he go under a pseudonym of a pseudonym. Mr. H. V. Yonge it was, this time—precisely the initials of his true name. The author of *Blindness, Living, Caught, Loving, Back, Concluding* and *Nothing* (to be published here in March) rose up from his chair in all of his names to greet his visitor, revealing himself. to be the owner of a typically tall, slender, slightly stoop-shouldered British figure.

What did one call Mr. Green this time—Mr. Yonge? (Mr. Green it was.) What did one talk about to Mr. Green? There were hedges and fences—to use the antique property term—crisscrossing about Mr. Green, and to hop over them was surely to trespass. Perhaps one talked only weather and water. (Ah! the weather was fine, and the baths were many during the crossing.) Nevertheless, the meeting turned out splendidly. Mr. Green, courteous, warm, conversational and unabashed, took his guest by the hand and led him across the difficult early passages.

"Say," he said, "I am the son of a prominent industrialist. Say, I am an engineer in the firm, who up to now has been unable to make money out of his books (that's thirty bloody years; I started when I was fifteen), and who has developed a technique for writing one hour every evening. Having been in industry for twenty-three years—and having written one hour every night during that time—I now have the opportunity for big money in my business. Large money in England and the United States is not paid to the novelist. And I do not want to interfere with my opportunities as a successful industrialist by revealing who I am."

Mr. Green was too intelligent to think he had satisfied his readers' curiosity. Nevertheless, obviously feeling he had said enough on that score, he took another line. "The great thing in life," he said, "is to get yourself right—not your health, but your brain. (May I take you on? Do you mind?) And I found quite early that I can only get myself right by writing. In other words, a kind of mental diarrhea, do you see? And I found, and I believe, that the only happiness in life is by self-expression. Oh, yes, there's married life, and children, but there's something beyond that I think—and I've been married twenty-two years. The expression of one's self which I still believe is writing, but which Mr. John Doe—that's what he is here, isn't it? —may have by gardening or by fishing.

"And so I found my happiness in life not through earning my living or through gardening or fishing but through writing. And I employ it as a kind of solitary self-control which has now, to my considerable embarrassment, made me an object of interest outside my own country. Being a person to whom not very much has happened in his life, having always been in easy circumstances, et cetera, I believe that the true life has nothing to do with sudden death, the atom bomb, et cetera."

Here Mr. Green paused, thought, smiled, studied his studier. "Do, do this," he said after a while, "if you possibly can. I believe that when things are named they're named by the people, some individual, some genius at naming things. And you'll find they always name the biggest things with the smallest names. Like the horrible cat-o-nine tails in England. The people called it pussy. How awful! And yet that's what's good about it. Now the H-bomb isn't going to be called the Hell-bomb. That's not it. That's too big. It's all wrong. I think I have a name: the tom-tit bomb! What do you think? Something small and terribly tiny for that monstrous bomb—the tom-tit bomb."

Maybe that was it. But would Mr. Green go back to a point he was making just prior to his most interesting divagation? "Ah, yes," Mr. Green said with a touch of regret, albeit amiably, "the true life has nothing to do with sudden death and great tragedy, and as such, as a writer, I do not consider that the field of the novel is concerned with major (international) issues. Rightly or wrongly, having arrived at this decision—I particularly emphasize this, as I do not criticize any novelist's work which is not on my own lines—I consider that the novel should be concerned with the everyday mishaps of ordinary life."

Mr. Green paused for breathing. "If that is so," he went on with unostentatious but inexorable logic, "it follows that I have to establish my characters in their situations in the first thirty pages, or eighth part of my novel. In English law a practitioner can't depart from his opening statement. I have to make my opening statement and for the remaining seven-eighths of the novel revolve around it, which may make me a minor writer, but which, upon consideration, may be the modern outcome as compared to the Victorians and the great novelists of persecution."

By the great novelists of persecution Mr. Green undoubtedly meant the Russians. And there was Tolstoy, for one, whose novels dealt with the everyday mishaps, but dealt as well with sudden death and great tragedy. "Tolstoy, of course, wrote about the vast issues of his time," Mr. Green said. "But that's what I mean by the modern outcome. He couldn't do it today. Take my country, historically speaking. The young men of my age were writing about the Spanish civil war. They've all changed their politics since then and have gotten caught up.

"The great issues should be dealt with by the poets, but I think [Mr. Green laughed] the great issues are the personal ones. How are you going to put the hydrogen bomb into prose? You've got to close your heart to something in this world, now don't you? As a matter of fact, the mantle has fallen on your shoulders in America, and we can sit back and watch with detachment. The responsibility isn't ours. It's yours, and we can now see how you jolly well run the world. Why should the novelist in Britain do anything about it? We now can have a delicious sense of irresponsibility. But even for Americans, with their full sense of responsibilty (due to the preponderance of power), it isn't for them to use that kind of thing in art. The realm of high politics isn't the concern of art. You see, I think these terrible weapons are high politics and not moral at all." Mr. Green summed up, undogmatically as it were: "It's a point of view, at any rate."

Apparently Americans had liked the fruits of the point of view. Whether it was an air of muted mystery that Mr. Green had managed from his everyday happenings to ordinary people, or whether it was not, *Loving* had won him many readers. Mr. Green didn't admit to feeling excessive excitement over his sudden popularity. "Been writing too long a time," he said in explanation, and then, leaning closer, in what can only be described as an enthusiastic half-whisper, he said: "Tell you the man I want to have read my books more than anybody else: Faulkner! Think he might have? Like to meet him more than anybody else." (Mr. Faulkner was only a half mile away at the time.)

The meeting did take place the following evening. Mr. Green spent twenty minutes with Mr. Faulkner. Mr. Green, tall, animated, urbane; Mr. Faulkner, small, patient, innocent. Mr. Green talked: Mr. Faulkner listened.

"Oh, he's a great man," Mr. Green said later. "I've never been so paralyzed in my life."

February 19, 1950

ELIZABETH BOWEN

THE author of *The Cocktail Party* once said that intelligence was rare. It is; and much rarer than we casually think it is. What the classical Mr. Eliot had in mind was the kind of pure intelligence that is experienced in Aristotle, Coleridge and Matthew Arnold. Well, Elizabeth Bowen, who is visiting us for the first time in seventeen years, has that kind of intelligence. It is the most noticeable, if not the most notable, thing about her—an alive, inevitable, inexhaustible intelligence that cannot help inform her speech with fresh and pertinent and engaging perceptions.

What's more, what's even better, this intelligence is complemented by a womanliness, or perhaps just a humanness, that in an intellectual person makes the totality rarer even than that day in June. Aside from this, secondarily as it were, Miss Bowen is Anglo-Irish, fifty, tall and strong and strong-boned, with a handsomely severe head that is a little reminiscent of the ascetic, formidable heads of the early Italian sculptures.

Miss Bowen's talk flows and has a quality of improvisation and discovery about it. "I have this terrifically recharged effect that coming here has on one," she said. "It's like contact with another intelligence that—this sounds rather oozy—happens in a love affair. I wish I could move around endlessly. Here I seem

to find a very natural atmosphere. It must be because I'm a sort
of hybrid. My ancestor was a Welshman who joined the Crom-
wellian army. It was all discreditable.

"I have a shot of New York," she said, "an idea of a big
intact city not bombed. The idea of intactness is a tremendously
exciting thing. But, then, the effect of growth and construction
has the same effect as destruction. It has the same wounds. A
bombed site and a clearing site have the same effect of terrible
ruin and give one a sort of convulsive feeling."

Miss Bowen talked about Cyril Connolly (one of her many
friends) and said she admired most his imaginary conversations
(demolitions really) with enemies (victims). They were imagined and verbal, and Miss Bowen wished he would write them.
"Virginia Woolf said to me," she related, "that a writer ought
to write at least a page a day, just as a pianist exercises every
day. When I consider—what is it?—how my days are spent, I
feel awfully bad about the days gone down the drain. I regret
I never kept a diary or a daily record."

Miss Bowen was here to visit, but she was also in the middle
of work. "I'm doing at the moment a very odd book, a small
piece of social history, of the Shelbourne Hotel in Ireland. One
could hardly call it the Ritz of Ireland, but it is the dominating
hotel, the moral and sociological dominating one. It has a curious history. It is a great subject really, but I want to write it off
so I can get into a novel. Though I do get kindled by it. In the
middle of the rising in 1916, people kept pouring into the place
for tea. In a queer way it is a face-saving thing, just as in the
middle of an air raid women would powder their faces. It's not
courage, but the way in which people survive."

Miss Bowen said she was fascinated but didn't "feel strong"
on that kind of book. "I feel happiest, in the sense of poetic
truth, in the short story. Yet if I wrote only short stories, I
should feel I was shirking. The novel is more of an ethical

thing. The short story has the dangers of perfection. Of course, there should be in the novel both the perfections: the sort of architectural proportions and the poetic truth—which are most possible in the short story.

"I suppose you must in a novel bite off more than you can chew. It's not that the short story is easy, but it is more a direct impulse, comes from a direct impression, a visible impression that is a sort of psychological flutter of the nerves. *Madame Bovary* does have perfection. But that's an obvious choice. If I had to reread any of my work with that sort of pure pleasure— and I do not mean self-satisfaction—it would be half a dozen stories. Not that I want to go back on the novels, but when I reread them I seem to find some sort of slimy tracts of myself, which I don't find in the stories."

Miss Bowen isn't at one with those writers who feel litera- ture is downhill today. "There are good sides in England now," she said. "One is the translations from the minority languages that are coming in. Another is the hallucinated kind of writing that Henry Green and William Sansom stand for. Perhaps hal- lucinated is the wrong word. I mean really visionary, the D. H. Lawrence of *The Fox* come to the surface again, a highly indi- vidual interpretation of things.

"The tradition of quaintness is being bogged down and the upper bourgeois idea is so useless now. The writers today, the good ones, don't have any sort of outfit and really write from the outside, as outsiders."

March 26, 1950

CHRISTINE WESTON

～

IN TRYING to describe Christine Weston—whose novel *The World Is a Bridge* was published the other week and which novel successfully tempted E. M. Forster from out his Cambridge fastness—the word "comely" keeps insisting itself; and though it is a fitting enough word, it can hardly be considered a descriptive one. Yet "comely" has a rare-metal ring to it, a sense of a time past and another kind of beauty that was seemly rather than awesome, and that, of course, is it: Mrs. Weston's attractiveness appeals to the intelligence rather than to the senses, and to the senses only afterward, and very subtly. Mrs. Weston, then, is a comely woman, in her middle-forties, is simple, forthright and gentle, though not sentimental.

Mrs. Weston was born in India, as her father before her (he was in the British Service), and as were both sets of her grandparents. Sitting at a table in the bar of a midtown hotel, Mrs. Weston talked a little about her "native" land. "Except for a few brief intervals," she said, "I was in India from the time I was born to the time I was married in 1923. I married an American from Cambridge. We went back to India in 1947. It was quite wonderful at the time, though in some ways it was very sad."

Why had Mrs. Weston felt sad? Hadn't it been the time of

India's triumph? "Yes," Mrs. Weston said, "it was a time of triumph. That, of course, didn't make me sad. What did, was going back to my old stamping grounds—the places where I'd been as a child and, of course, you develop illusions about those places."

Then Mrs. Weston had been happy as a child—wasn't that the logical conclusion? "I was exceedingly happy," Mrs. Weston replied. "And going back, and seeing those things—well, everything was a little different." She laughed, adding "a little dustier, a little rustier."

"We went to Delhi to witness the 'transference' (I think they called it). It was very stirring. We saw Nehru, whom I think a very great man. Part of his problem is for him to remain a person aside from being a great world figure. When he speaks on world affairs, he speaks as you and I speak. That's been so hard for people to take. We've all been accustomed to generalities, insincerity and soothing syrup."

Mrs. Weston nodded at her husband. "He's a great sportsman," she said matter-of-factly. "We were careful not to horn in on anything. What we did do was to go into the countryside for walking and hunting. It gave us a chance to get behind the scenes. We had been warned not to go, but we had nothing except kindness and affection and hospitality.

"The novel covers the period when I was there, the time of partition. But it was something else again when I wrote *Indigo*, and it's something that interests me as a writer. I wrote that book almost from memory; I had been away twenty years, you know. After returning, it was very strange, and very nice, to find how accurately my memory had functioned. You might say that it is an example of how important the impressions of childhood are. I suppose it wells up from one's own subconscious and unsubconscious.

That last was an interesting word. Mrs. Weston laughed not

at all immodestly. "It *is* interesting," she said, "and maybe it's good. I don't know. But it's funny. I remember I used to say a *spilt* personality."

Mrs. Weston returned, associatively as it were, to children. "One of the wonderful things about being brought up in India," she said, "is the stimulating effect it has on the imagination. It's true, for example, of Jim Corbett's children—you know, the man who wrote *Man-eaters*. They have contact with the Indian children, with the land, with animals, and it's a simple sort of life that even the well-to-do are brought up on. There are no synthetic distractions. You have to make your own amusements. There is no social life except for what is invented by one's self. There is a chance to grow up that way; there's something fresh in that life."

She turned her mind to literature. "Henry Green," she said, "is a breath of fresh air. I wish there were more like him." Mrs. Weston's husband agreed with an emphatic nod. "Funny thing," she continued, "my husband has read everything of Green's he could get hold of, but I don't think he's read one of my books. . . . Well, I don't think he has to. It's one of the unnecessary horrors of marriage."

Mr. Weston had been a forester for many years. Had Mrs. Weston ever forestered with him? "Yes, I used to do some timber inventory with him." Even though he hadn't read any of her books? "Yes, even so," Mrs. Weston said.

Had there been any coercion? "Well, there wasn't any good grace on my part," she said, with an affection that was even better than good grace.

April 16, 1950

CHARLES JACKSON

THE impression one gets on seeing Charles Jackson (whose *The Sunnier Side* has been intriguing readers for the past few weeks) is single—it's the sense unmistakably felt of the terrible and moving effort in the man to be deeply honest at each and every moment.

This is no mean thing—and one bows before the precarious spectacle. But such is the power of the urbane, routine day that, over the teacups (to quote Mr. Eliot), there comes that small talk of you and me. Over the coffee, though, the talk turned out to be not quite so small.

The stories in *The Sunnier Side*, Mr. Jackson's first try in the genre, were all written for the book, though some appeared in various periodicals. When he was asked about it, he said, "Writers talk so badly about their writing. I can tell you this much: what it really is is Don Birnam as a kid, with all the grimness and hilarity of kids. The stories have a continuity with the novels. They relate to the novel coming up."

Mr. Jackson has been working on a new novel for a year and a half now, and expects to see it published in 1952. "I have a long-range plan," he said, "and I want to keep on working in spite of hazards, Hollywood and emotional upsets. I have been able to bring something out every other year."

That is how it has been, starting with *The Lost Weekend*. Speaking of that famous adventure on Third Avenue, had Mr. Jackson been prepared for the book's extraordinary success? "I believed it would be successful," Mr. Jackson replied. "I believed in that book more than any since. I believed it was good. What I mean is it succeeds in doing what it set out to do."

When had Mr. Jackson gotten under way as a writer? "Oh, I had always written as a kid," he said. "When I was fourteen and fifteen I was writing poetry. When I'd finish a poem I'd look into the mirror to see if I looked different, if my face had changed. It's a tremendous thing—writing. I really felt sorry for my brother and sister for not knowing who or what was in their midst. When I was twenty-six or twenty-seven I knew then I had been a victim of adolescence. I knew I had to work at writing, that it was a full-time job and very hard. Of course, it was lots of fun, it was a circus, when I went to Hollywood and the 21 Club. But I should have been at my desk."

Mr. Jackson took a minute out, taking perspective as it were. "The hazards of success," he went on, "that's what I'm writing about. Imagine, someone sent Tennessee Williams the clippings on Arthur Miller. Imagine! Writers don't compete with each other.

"Only a year and a half ago did I realize what had happened to me as a result of *The Lost Weekend*—its ballooning to a success out of all proportion to its real value. You feel a fraud. I know that Thomas Heggen felt that way; he was scared to death. That's a pattern. I began to realize what had happened to me; it was utterly abnormal, and so I retrenched. That's what weakened *The Fall of Valor*. But enough is enough. You can let success be your finish. Most of the people you see don't read your books and don't care and it's a circus. So now I'm in New Hampshire, where it's dull as hell but where at least I'm working."

Mr. Jackson wasn't finished with it; his sensitivity and scrupulousness forced him back to his dismissal of Hollywood and the night-time cafés. "When I said enough is enough I didn't mean it as a generality. All of it, the playing around, the circus, is a part of experience, and that's all right. I don't mean to be snooty. Perhaps some writers can work that way, but I know where I belong is at my desk and not at the 21 Club. That's all I mean."

Mr. Jackson looked away, setting his face (unknowingly) a little tightly. "I'm getting tough about work," he declared. "Personalities don't count. You ride over them. Your devotion to your family should be equal to your devotion to your work—and, of course, they're always in conflict. The demands of your family come at the wrong time, or the demands of your work come at the wrong time." Mr. Jackson, having said it, dismissed it. "It's every writer's problem," he said, waving his hand.

Mr. Jackson once had another problem: he was awed by two people, Thomas Mann and Greta Garbo. He finally met Mann (through the solicitous arrangements of Mrs. Mann) and his first reaction was, "My God, I've got to get out of here." He didn't get out, and a friendship began that Mr. Jackson deeply respects. Mr. Mann, by the way, compared *The Lost Weekend* to Knut Hamsun's *Hunger* (one of Hamsun's best and sustained shorter novels). Mr. Jackson met Garbo too, at Charlie Chaplin's. But, he insists, he's still pretty scared of her.

April 30, 1950

ROBERT NATHAN

~~

SINCE Robert Nathan is the successful author of more than twenty-five novels, among them *One More Spring, Portrait of Jennie* and *The River Journey*, it is not at all, therefore, a much of a muchness when he publishes a book of poems. In his middle fifties, he has forsaken prose for poetry only a few times, and so it was news when his newest book of poetry (entitled *The Green Leaf*) made its appearance a few weeks ago. It was, too, not at all a coincidence that Mr. Nathan turned up at a plushy midtown restaurant just about the time this reporter wandered in.

Mr. Nathan, let it be said, has urbanity, but not the typical kind—that is, the typical kind that is aloof and suave and un-ruffled. Mr. Nathan, though he doesn't at all ruffle, has the kind that doesn't exclude anger. He is also faintly and hand-somely touched with what one might call world-weariness.

Mr. Nathan looked about him (though he was profoundly indoors) and spoke of outdoors. "I remember," he said, really remembering, "Park Avenue having the clop-clop of horses, of horse-drawn milk wagons. It was nice. Now—the traffic! Two years from today traffic will get into such a snarl that for blocks no man or vehicle will move, they won't be able to untangle it, and they'll have to build a street over it."

Mr. Nathan's pause was one for emphasis. "And the city has gotten awfully shabby. Speaking of this shabbiness, it's the place, not the people. The women in New York are most attractive (I didn't notice them in Hollywood at all), most human, most womanly. But the place is shabby in a very curious way. The houses used to have a kind of glamour, of elegance."

Wasn't it that the city was older and tireder? Mr. Nathan would have none of it. "People don't seem to care any more," he said. "It's the triumph of the mass mind over the individual. No, I don't find anything exciting here except the people and mostly the women and they seem to be quite something—but in the first place there is a leveling-down at top speed. Where the most people are, there you will find the most leveling-down."

How did Mr. Nathan account for this Nathan's law? "Well," he said, "you get tired of keeping things up. Life gets more crowded and indifferent. You have to have a certain peace and leisure and elbow room in order to have a certain elegance. The thing we're in now looks more like a sardine can. It's a frightening thing to me. It's part of the war between the mass mind and the individual."

Did Mr. Nathan see any hope? "I'm getting pessimistic," he replied. "If you say the word 'elegance' today, you feel you must apologize for it. Thirty or forty years ago even the worker, or the most inelegant, wanted elegance. Today it's no one's dream. People still have the very human dream of distinction, in athletics, in beauty contests and radio quiz programs. They certainly none of them think in terms of manners, of graciousness or of dignity."

Hadn't Mr. Nathan spent some years, about seven, in Hollywood—and what about it? "The trouble with Hollywood," Mr. Nathan said promptly and with zest, "is that there are too many geniuses and not enough men of talent. A genius is a man who has had at least one big picture written, acted, directed and cut by other people. But it has to have grossed a great deal of money. If he has had *two* such pictures, he is a great genius and has what is known as his own touch and is an authentic genius."

And what had Mr. Nathan to say about the state of letters?

"Literature?" Mr. Nathan asked, and answered: "That's in a bad way. It follows the pattern of the cities; it has gotten shabbier and shabbier. But most of it is the fault of the critics. They write enthusiastically about dull and pornographic books. They are dangerous citizens. Now, let me say this: I was delighted with a book like Bunny Wilson's *Hecate County*. It had a literary approach; there was a life there. Or the Marquand *Point of No Return*. But the critics don't tell the bores what bores they are."

He smiled a little viciously. "People think me wishy-washy, a gentle and sentimental writer, and use the word whimsical on me. I'm about as whimsical as a scorpion." Mr. Nathan's laugh wasn't like Bela Lugosi's but it could have been Karloff's.

"In literature the critics admire only the unpleasant, the beastly, the dirty, the sordid. They don't like anything that isn't violent any more." Mr. Nathan paused, smiled, said, "Just call me Queen Victoria."

May 7, 1950

DYLAN THOMAS

～～

RECENTLY poets have manifested an increasing tendency toward respectability. They are presentable and well dressed. They hold responsible views on political matters and are the backbones of universities. They support their families. They have even gone into government. In cold weather they wear overcoats and for the rain they have rubbers. They seem to have accepted the dictum of the times (and Thomas Mann): the artist is strange enough inwardly, outwardly he should be anonymous. And so poets read their poems as if they were reading the Sunday newspaper to their wives over the boiled eggs. Interviewed, what they have to say is serious, cooperative and directly illuminating. Their poems may puzzle the public; the poets themselves are proving they are socially viable.

But when Dylan Thomas (pronounced Dillon) arrived on his first visit to America it was obvious that this revolution of respectability had left him "disengaged." The thirty-five-year-old Welsh poet—whose poems are as wild and structural as atoms and who is regarded by many critics to be the best young poet writing in English since the extraordinary debut of Wystan Hugh Auden—is one of a passing breed of spiritual anarchists who resist every encroachment of society merely by ignoring it.

Thomas, this observer feels, is a seriously elusive man. He is for chit-chat and verbal games and oblique counters. In social gatherings he gives the impression, fleetingly, of a wary animal of the woods who walks stolidly and boldly into the clearing. When he reads poetry (as everyone knows who has heard him), his wariness and his shyness and his stolidness fall away. His stirring and subtle and remarkably clean reading of poetry (read unashamedly as poetry) elicited from a critical listener the judgment, "This is the greatest reading since Yeats" (and, typically, from Thomas himself the comment, "I'm afraid it's second-rate Charles Laughton").

Thomas has just completed a reading tour of the nation that took in some forty university towns, winding up with a thumping reading for the Modern Museum poetry sessions under the direction of Lloyd Frankenberg. On May 15, by popular demand, he makes a farewell appearance at The Poetry Center of the Ninety-second Street Y which, under John Malcolm Brinnin, is chiefly responsible for Thomas' visit here. In celebration of this first "coming," New Directions is publishing this spring some selected poems (about twenty-six) in a limited, signed edition.

One day recently this writer met Dylan Thomas at a Third Avenue bar and grill. "I love Third Avenue," Thomas said, filled with genuine admiration (although the only other landmark he has really visited is the RCA building). "I don't believe New York," he went on. "It's obvious to anyone why. All the same, I believe in New Yorkers. Whether they've ever questioned the dream in which they live, I wouldn't know, because I won't ever dare ask that question."

Thomas is a little short, a little round and round-eyed, a little fair, very unruly-haired. His strongly modeled but no longer cherubic face (as Augustus John drew it) bears a male resemblance to Elsa Lanchester's. He said: "Say I am thirty-five years older, small, slim, dark, intelligent, and darting-doting-dotting-eyed. Say I am balding and toothlessing. I am also well-dressed." Mr. Thomas was wearing rumpled tweeds and was coatless. "Do you think that an invisible coat is well dressed? It is absolutely essential that I wear an invisible coat. Visible overcoats make you feel proprietorial."

Avoiding the sartorial question, I asked Thomas if he ever read American poetry. He replied with mock eloquence: "Whenever the day is dull and the rain is falling and the feet of the heron are battering against my window, and whenever the Garnetts (who are a literary family) or the gannets (who I believe are a bird) are gossiping in the bay, then what do I do but count my beads and then: a volume of American verse edited by Oscar Williams!"

What, one wanted to know, were Mr. Thomas' conclusions after such an immersion? "I suddenly have the death wish," he said, "which is what I started with. And then I have to read the poetry again and then I like it. And then it all begins again: the melancholy, gay, euphoric roundabout."

Thomas drank his whisky and beer a little moodily. "Any possible success that could happen to me is bad for me," he said, apparently thinking of his audiences. To pursue the thought: Was it "success" if people liked his work?

"If people like my poetry, if they like my reading of it, if they like me, that is success, and that is bad for me. I should be what I was," Mr. Thomas replied. Did Mr. Thomas mean thirty-five years ago? "No, twenty years ago," he said. "Then I was arrogant and lost. Now I am humble and found. I prefer that other."

May 14, 1950

ALDOUS HUXLEY

THE author of the recently published collection of essays
entitled *Themes and Variations* (the same author of *Crome
Yellow, Antic Hay, Those Barren Leaves, Point Counter Point,
Brave New World, Eyeless in Gaza, Ends and Means, After
Many a Summer,* as well as some two dozen other books) sat
low in his low chair, his imposingly long legs extended and
crossed at the ankles. Position to the contrary, Aldous Huxley
was not altogether relaxed—not at first anyway. Later, yes; but
then, no.

Mr. Huxley was waiting around for his visitor to say something. His visitor, contemplating the Huxlian erudition, said
nothing. Instead of talking, he was thinking: "Huxley knows so
much, there is nothing to talk to him about." Yet the moment
wasn't altogether anxious. There were, after all, Mr. Huxley's
comfortably long legs, and—what was more patent than the
erudition—Mr. Huxley's excellent manners and his quiet and
mature charm.

All of which came to the rescue of the reasonably rescuable
situation. "God, it's awful!" Mr. Huxley said. "I know how
you feel working on a literary supplement and seeing so many
books day after day. I used to work on the old *Athenaeum*—
that was about thirty years ago. [Mr. Huxley will celebrate his

fifty-fourth birthday in July.] I remember going into the office and seeing the flood of books, and each morning it would rise some six inches. People who found literary reviews," Mr. Huxley said by way of association, "feel an extraordinary kind of self-congratulation. They feel they're much more important than the people who write books. They have a feeling of being saints."

Mr. Huxley may have been filling silence, but he was also warming up. "It's a fascinating subject altogether," he said, "the hypocrisy of the esthetic life. There's a real cant, isn't there? It's a new phenomenon, but I suppose it existed verbally in the ancient world. I imagine Alexandria must have been very like New York: the fantastic mixture of people and the same kind of extreme intellectual sophistication and preoccupation with literary forms."

Mr. Huxley passed some of his articulateness on to his visitor, who was at last able to ask Mr. Huxley what Mr. Huxley was up to, besides being on the verge of leaving for Europe. "For a long time," Mr. Huxley said, "I have been thinking of doing the impossible job of writing a historical novel, and I've been thinking of collecting my material on the spot. It would be fourteenth-century Italy. It fascinates me. Why! Well, it has the fascination of the impossible task—I still don't know how it's to be done—of indicating that people are always the same and awfully different."

Why did fourteenth-century Italy fascinate Mr. Huxley? "It's awfully good," he said. "It's really human nature with the lid off of it. It really is wonderful. The violence and picturesqueness; and I must say it's fun when one reads a life of the Middle Ages and the intimate life emerges. All kinds of things that we regard as very, very strange they took for granted. There is that passage from extreme sanctity to extreme brutality—things we consider incompatible go on in the same breath. Men ate off gold plate and were monstrously filthy. Beautiful women painted their teeth, which ate away the enamel. [Mr. Huxley said "et" away.] Women made themselves so revolting that the men were driven to sodomy. No, I must say it's fascinating— and then you get into the early humanists: Petrarch, Boccaccio and that extraordinary woman, St. Catherine, rushing about and bawling out the Pope."

Mr. Huxley was silent for a while and then said he had a long novelette in mind, too. It may, he added, turn into a full-length novel. Would it turn out (one hoped) another *Antic Hay?* "That was rather fun," Mr. Huxley said gaily. "But it came after World War I, and it couldn't be written again."

The gentle and tranquil-looking author considered the reasons for his statement. "No, I don't think so," he said. "One is, after all, thirty years older. One has, in his post-adolescence, a burst of astonishment at life. Everything seems amusing and extraordinary and amazing. And then not again."

Did Mr. Huxley—who had transposed music into the dimensions of fiction so remarkably well—did he listen to music these days? "Oh, yes," Mr. Huxley replied. "I'm still very fond of music and I'm delighted by the long-playing records."

How did he find California? "I like it," Mr. Huxley said. "I'm very fond of the climate. And I'm very fond of the desert, both in California and New Mexico. The magnificence of clouds coming over the mountains!" Mr. Huxley shook his head in admiration.

New Mexico painters were always overwhelmed by their vistas and colors, weren't they? Mr. Huxley nodded. "Perhaps the only great landscape painter was Turner—he could paint anything. When you get into the desert—the shadows of the clouds!—it is overwhelming, and it must be admitted that the desert is often in appalling taste. I imagine no one except some extraordinary, eccentric genius like Turner could paint it."

Thinking of the New Mexican painters (and the Californian ones, if there were any), Mr. Huxley smiled. "Nowhere," he said, "is hell so paved with good intentions as in art."

May 21, 1950

ROBERT PENN WARREN

IT WAS Nietzsche who said that perhaps all vulgarity consisted in man's inability to resist stimuli. Well, too often and too glibly we get an impression of a human being, and then we're in for a bit of a shock. That's what happened to this reporter when he met Robert Penn Warren the other day in the bar of a quiet midtown hotel. Only in this case the eventual shock was rewarding and all to the good.

Holding a glass of iced tea in his muscular hand, Mr. Warren —who is the author of *World Enough and Time,* and is one of America's most distinguished novelists, poets, critics and teachers—stared neutrally at his guest. Beneath the dulled rust-red, short-clipped hair his face was astonishingly compact: slits of eyes almost lashless, taut skin over hard cheekbones, spare modeled nose, straight line of mouth—the "entire consort" a sculpture in granite. The hard-knit, barrel-chested torso added more, if that were possible, to the impression. But when Mr. Warren talked, the shock was the discovery in each subsequent moment of how much warmth and wit and wisdom, of how much humanity, there issued from that stony image.

The forty-five-year-old Kentuckian, it turned out, was not an author to talk about his new book, though he did refer to it once as "this crime." Back a way, Mr. Warren had written that he regarded a study of Faulkner to be the greatest challenge to modern criticism. "Well," he said quickly, "criticism missed him. There was a fashionable liberalism—as opposed to the real thing—and it wrote Faulkner off as politically bad, and a whole generation missed him. And now you meet them—people with no background for him and yet the furious impact he makes on them is a marvel. There's been a whole lag on Faulkner, based on a too-political criticism."

One knew it well—the insistence on reading literature as though it were a tract, and the dismissal of every formal element in a work of the imagination. "They don't even get the politics in Faulkner," Mr. Warren said with a touch of passion, "let alone the other—the tonality, the rhythms, the texture. They make an even more horrendous error than that; they insist on a political interpretation and then misunderstand the doctrine!"

One knew that Mr. Warren would teach Faulkner (and Coleridge and Blake, two of his favored moderns) scrupulously, but what with the success of *All the King's Men* in all its aspects —as novel, play and film—and of the new novel (a Literary Guild selection), would Mr. Warren teach again? "I intend to teach," Mr. Warren replied. "I'm on leave this fall. I've been teaching sort of on a two-fourths basis. [Mr. Warren's *I've* is a very soft *Ah've.*] There are very fundamental compensations in teaching if you're in the right kind of place and have the right kind of students.

"I think the academic process, although on one side it has its comic aspects, on the other produces truly profound and humanistic people who serve as a sort of buffer against the jittery, fashionable kind of thing. A university has the failures and defects of institutions, just like government or the family or anything else. But I do think it gives certain perspectives in its better reaches that you'd not get if you were outside. The question doesn't come up in teaching, but it does in writing—

whether it is a worthwhile activity: Is it really something to do? Is it a serious thing for a grown-up man to do? That sort of questioning today blanks out a lot of fellows."

Mr. Warren *was* going to keep on writing? "Yup," Mr. Warren said. "I've got my plans. I don't know what's going to come of them. I generally carry a couple of novels around in me. I'm also trying to revise the verse play of *All the King's Men* for publication, and I'm at work on a long poem, based on an episode in American history, which may be a verse play or a poem of voices. I have to carry things around for so long that they're all overlapping."

Would Mr. Warren "unlap" for a moment and talk about the new verse play? Mr. Warren would. "It has to do with two sons of Charles Lewis, who was related to Meriwether and married to Thomas Jefferson's sister. The sons became involved in a perverse, violent and hideous situation, out West in Kentucky. One Lewis opened up the West, and two Lewises were devoured by it."

Mr. Warren considered his future poem. "Jefferson," he said, "was a kind of foster father to Lewis; he will be the chorus of the piece. The great libertarian founder of our country will have to face this terrible thing in his own blood. What I've written are just fragments. I haven't solved the basic style for it yet. But I hope to get things assembled and then I will try to make the big push."

June 25, 1950

WILBUR DANIEL STEELE

IT WAS with considerable and unmixed pleasure that this reporter went off to meet Wilbur Daniel Steele. The reason was not only that Mr. Steele's newest novel, *Diamond Wedding,* had just been published by Doubleday. He remembered his youthful days when he had gone on a protracted reading bout—belatedly, it was true. But Mr. Steele's short stories, then very popular, had been a source of immense excitement and value. One was, naturally, grateful.

Mr. Steele, it turned out, was sixty-four, medium tall, bony and slight. He was profoundly shy. It was not a shyness that you eventually overcame; it was shyness forever—and one had to accept that. After all, Mr. Steele was now sixty-four: what he was, he was—and shyness, in his case, was not an embellishment. The silence was present as a continuous and concrete thing, and it was broken only by effort.

There had been in Mr. Steele's life a kind of pause, hadn't there? "For quite a while there was," Mr. Steele said. "I wasted about seven years of my life, as quite a lot of other writers. I had a mix-up with the theatre. Besides, my type of story, my generation of story had gone radically out of style. I thought the story had gotten better, but I didn't seem to be able to get the hang of it."

Would Mr. Steele elaborate on this idea that the short story had changed? "I was about the last gasp of an epoch," he said. How would Mr. Steele characterize the story of the last gasp? "It was a plot story," he said. "It was a constructed story. Then there came in the episode story and the rough boys." What did Mr. Steele mean by the rough boys? Mr. Steele thought and finally came up with what was on the tip of his tongue. "Hemingway," he said suddenly. "Hemingway was the first of them."

A silence then. Mr. Steele broke it. "I'm a very bad one to talk about letters," he said neutrally, without innuendo. "I've been cooped into myself, I'm afraid. I seldom get off my place [Lyme, Connecticut]. This is the first time I've been in New York in a year." Didn't Mr. Steele miss Broadway? "I do not," he said unneutrally. "I'm miserable in New York. I was in New York for two winters and, my God, I walked the dog and looked into store windows. That was my New York."

And now Mr. Steele didn't have to walk the dog? "No, sir," he said. "There's only one house in sight. It's ideal for me. I do my homework and then work on the place. The other day I mowed the lawn and that's five miles of walking. And over rocks." Mr. Steele groaned with pleasure. What was the homework like? "All my life," he replied, "I've worked in the mornings, religiously from half-past eight to half-past one."

Mr. Steele stared into space, then went on. "Writing is very hard work," he said. "Harder than for anybody else." For anybody else? "Yes, sir," he said. "I think I hold the record. To put a sentence together is like climbing a mountain range. I really mean it."

The next question was so ineluctable that one had to subdue its fortissimo: why (one suppressed "in Heaven's name") did Mr. Steele write? Mr. Steele replied straightforwardly enough. "It's the only God's way I can make a living," he said. "I'd be utterly useless doing anything else." What about when Mr.

Steele started out—it wasn't a money motive then, was it? "Well, writing was just as hard then," Mr. Steele answered. "I always wanted to write, and I always liked to be about to write, but it was like pick and shovel work. You see, I was studying to be an illustrator in Paris. I thought I'd better write a short story and sell it and thus get to illustrate it."

But there must have been some other motive—some interior push. Mr. Steele replied with a touch of correctness: "After all, I'm a professional writer." As a professional writer, did Mr. Steele attempt to amuse the reader? What was the end of the writing anyway? "I don't know," Mr. Steele said. "I sometimes think I'm the other way—I write what I feel. One thing, of course, is that I'm lazy as hell—and if it had not been for my having made a practice of working four to five hours a day, seven days a week, fifty-two weeks a year——" Mr. Steele clenched his fists in tight, knotty balls. "Mostly I'm that way because I'm not getting anywhere when I'm working. There is a wall between me and words. The difficulty to express myself keeps me always fighting."

This fighting, one volunteered, might create a tension in Mr. Steele's work, might give to it the drama that made it exciting. Mr. Steele said nothing. It might, mightn't it? one persisted.

"It might," Mr. Steele said, and nodded his head in agreement.

August 6, 1950

BUDD SCHULBERG

USUALLY, when you think of the progress of writers, it moves from east to west. In Budd Schulberg's case it was different: he grew up out West and, as he himself says, "I worked my way east."

Born in New York in 1914, Mr. Schulberg migrated to the movie capital when he was a stripling of four, his father being head of Paramount at the time. Hollywood was home for him until he moved off to prep school and Dartmouth. For a while he went back to the celluloid city as a kind of writing utility out-fielder, then to Dartmouth just to live. Besides just living, he wrote *What Makes Sammy Run.* In the service for four years, he settled in Pennsylvania in 1946 and came up with *The Harder They Fall.* Now he's got *The Disenchanted;* and if he doesn't look out, in an inning or two, another novel to be exact, he'll have hit for the hat trick—which, in baseball, means hitting a single, double, triple and home run in one game.

The thirty-six-year-old Mr. Schulberg is a sensitive and gentle companion. In fact, his gentleness transforms itself into an exacting concern with the modulations of an idea—such shadings and qualifications lending to Mr. Schulberg's speech a hesitant and touchingly tormented character. At the same time, within this muted atmosphere that Mr. Schulberg can't help but create, there exists an awareness in his companions that Mr. Schulberg is possessed of a remarkably powerful chest, that he is, as well, the proud possessor of a promising prize fighter—all of which combines into a nice paradox.

Naturally, the talk gravitated to Hollywood and to its awesome powers. "At times I'm misunderstood about Hollywood," Mr. Schulberg said in his muted way. "They [by *they,* Mr. Schulberg presumably meant Hollywoodians] think I'm all anti-Hollywood, but I'll probably write about it more. It's—it's kind of my Salinas Valley. It's my material and I'm trying to understand it; and of course I'm not at all afraid to do it as honestly as I can and that's confused with muckraking and exposés, which I'm not interested in doing."

Could one say outright that the Halliday of *The Disenchanted* was Scott Fitzgerald? Mr. Schulberg considered the question. "You could say something like this," he said. "It's true that I've made up a list of the writers who achieved something in the Twenties and then lost their way and went off on difficult tangents. I think I stopped at twelve." Mr. Schulberg paused, as much to let that fact sink in as to gather further momentum. "And though Halliday may seem like Fitzgerald, actually he partakes of a dozen writers I knew, all of whom had been figures in the Twenties and had later on gone to Hollywood. They had talent and got short-circuited."

Mr. Schulberg's voice barely carried over the muffled sound of ice in short glasses. "This I saw all my life," he said. "My father had quite an appreciation of writing. He was a kind of frustrated writer and I think he was drawn by the more literary kind of writers, many of whom were very exciting for me, as a young kid, to meet, very stimulating. Then, ten years later, to find them dull and talking the way they did and nothing produced."

A longer pause than before, then Mr. Schulberg: "A disease

for which Hollywood happens to be a convenient symbol. There were Hollywoods before Hollywood was even discovered. There were people who went there and met it on its own terms and beat it." Did Mr. Schulberg have anyone in mind? "Well, Faulkner. Even the movie scripts he did are good work. I admire the way he does a stint and then goes back to his own roots. It isn't a hell from which you can't escape. The challenge of doing a good movie, of doing a good piece of work, isn't something to be ashamed of. The only thing to be ashamed of is to be sucked in and to let yourself be dependent on that contract and pay check. That's when you're lost."

They were lost and they were disenchanted—which brought back the tragic Halliday. Mr. Schulberg in *The Disenchanted* had gotten into even Scott Fitzgerald's remarkable prose. Wasn't that something of a departure? "I had to break through the style I had established for myself," Mr. Schulberg said with sobriety. "A hard-boiled style like *Sammy* can be limiting. Also, I began to feel that a number of very good writers, really very good writers, were falling short of greatness because style had become a strait jacket for their emotions and ideas, and in meeting them and talking to them I thought how much better they are than their work—even though the work was damn good. Among writers there is a fear of erudition and ideas, a fear really to show one's self. There is a real frontier thing here," said Mr. Schulberg with a querulousness, a tentativeness, that could only be polite.

November 5, 1950

JOHN DOS PASSOS

EVER since *Three Soldiers* (almost thirty years ago) and *Manhattan Transfer* (twenty-five years ago), John Dos Passos has been taped as one of a half-dozen leading novelists in this thriving nation of novelists. Mr. Dos Passos continues to be a novelist: he is one-third through a novel right now. Nevertheless, the novelist has given us plenty of nonfiction works, including *Journey Between Wars, State of the Nation* and *The Prospect Before Us.*

"It seems to be a regular pattern," Mr. Dos Passos said, referring to his imaginative and reportorial alternations. "As soon as I had done *Three Soldiers* I did some journalism, and so it's been all my life. I've been working on a long essay on Jefferson and doing a great deal of research. *That's* a departure, because God knows I have to learn to do research."

Mr. Dos Passos laughed, not nervously, but with suddenness. That "suddenness" was the strange element in Mr. Dos Passos: after a question, he would be silent for a quiet moment and then suddenly answer with an energetic burst ("Yez," he would say, exploding the word swiftly, or "Oh, yes," loud and almost startled) and then settle into conventional conversation.

Leading Mr. Dos Passos gently into fiction, one asked the fifty-four-year-old author if he had reread *Manhattan Transfer*

143

recently. "Not for a long time," Mr. Dos Passos replied. "I did run through it with agony for a Modern Library edition. There's not much point in going over the old stuff. You can't do anything about it unless you're rewriting like George Moore used to do. But then if you did that you wouldn't have time for your new stuff."

What was Mr. Dos Passos up to in his reportage? "I've been trying a big-term experiment," he said. "I've been trying to get a series of written photographs of institutions as they develop. These various trips I take, I sort of keep one question in mind: what sort of institutions are appearing and how do they affect people? I try to start with a blank page each time as far as it is possible. I try to discard notions of what is desirable and undesirable."

Had Mr. Dos Passos experienced a reality canceling out some of his beliefs? "Yes," he said, "oh, yes! I was very much for British socialism, but when I returned in 1947 it seemed to me more of a new lid clamped down on a crowded island. Of course, the Conservative lid had been fitting rather badly."

Was the choice limited to only those two lids? "No," said Mr. Dos Passos, "the old one is completely worn out. I've come to question whether it's possible for people to change the trend of a society that is developing in an undesirable way. Of course, I still think it is." Mr. Dos Passos considered the problem. "The great genius of the British," he said, "is the way in which they carry on their enormous changes with a minimum of destruction, which is a very valuable thing. But the fact that someone takes over on top doesn't necessarily change the form of society. That's no different than a change in the board of directors of steel. Change should start from the bottom and work up instead of from up to down. But, of course, the whole tendency of great hierarchical structures is to get people to depend on that very hierarchy."

In this context, how did Mr. Dos Passos find America? "The whole picture is much more fluid," Mr. Dos Passos said. "It's far more encouraging than in England. Take the fact of farming: in the Twenties farming seemed coming to a dead end; the old family farm seemed to be able to go no further. Now it's very exciting and full of opportunities for people."

Did Mr. Dos Passos feel that he held an advantage over the straight reporter? "Well," Mr. Dos Passos said, "there are hundreds of ways of doing things and all can be valuable—but presumably a novelist can go a little deeper. Think of all the verbiage about the Negro. But no one has said anything more permanently illuminating than Faulkner."

In spite of Mr. Dos Passos' feelings, Faulkner had been criticized for his political ideas. "Oh, well," Mr. Dos Passos said with utter and quiet assurance, "in my day we had the old stuffies. Today we have the new stuffies. When I look back I prefer the old stuffies who at least had a taste for style. The new stuffies have only their prejudices."

November 12, 1950

W. SOMERSET MAUGHAM AND
EVELYN WAUGH

THE justification for the double talk is that Somerset Maugham and Evelyn Waugh both are revisits: Mr. Maugham and Mr. Waugh revisited. The justification for talking with them at all is that both are fair writers. A couple of .350 hitters. You just can't ignore that kind of prowess. Both, it turned out, too, touched on the theme of pleasure—each in his own way.

"Some books," Mr. Maugham said with an urbanity that was not at all disconcerting, "are written in anguish, others just write themselves—and those are jolly to write." One knew the exemplars: *Of Human Bondage* was written in pain, *Cakes and Ale* was written with pleasure. Mr. Maugham smiled, and added: "And parts of *The Razor's Edge* were written in ease and parts in difficulty." Mr. Maugham leaned toward his visitor ever so slightly; it was just enough of an emphasis. "But d'you know," he said, "even when a thing is difficult, if you are a writer you are never so happy as when you are writing."

There were writers—Thomas Mann, for instance—who would not agree. "I know there are," Mr. Maugham said. "I can only say I wrote stories because it was a delight to write them. There are always snags and you worry about them, but then you circumvent them and go on. I can only say that when I was in the full flush of my vigor [Mr. Maugham will celebrate his seventy-fifth birthday in January] I had far more stories in me than I ever had time to write. And y'know, to mention the book critics who are so down on Hemingway, they are very unfair. They must know a writer has his ups and downs. I think myself that *Père Goriot* is the most readable of all novels, but Balzac was inconceivably bad at times. Someone like Dostoevsky was very up and down." Mr. Maugham summed up: "People who are always on a level, shall we say, are rather mediocre."

An earnest question: What was Mr. Maugham writing? "I am not writing any more novels or stories or plays," he said with an alarming touch of positiveness. "I am devoting the rest of my life to writing essays, a form that has always interested me and that no one is writing any more and that I can do for my own pleasure and satisfaction."

Last time this reporter visited Mr. Waugh, Mr. Waugh was attacking his own book—it was the hilarious *Scott-King's Modern Europe*—against the defense of it by his visitor. Since then Mr. Waugh has a new novel, *Helena*. He said, "Hah! It has to be the other way round now. I consider it an absolute masterpiece. You'll have to do all the attacking." "Attecking" was the way Mr. Waugh said it, all the while gazing at his visitor in owlish fashion. (Hah! But the visitor couldn't atteck it because he hadn't read it.)

Why was *Helena* a masterpiece? "Well," Mr. Waugh said, "it's never been done before. Nearest thing to it is E. M. Forster's sketches of Alexandria. They're unrecognized masterpieces, but they're disconnected and very short.

"You see," Mr. Waugh said, "my book has a whole series of themes. It's the story of a woman's life. Then there's the split between East and West, which is almost topical. Then there's the whole theme of conversion. It has a great deal of humor, too, my book has, and jokes. Sort of family jokes. It has some very funny passages. It's a broad humor, but there's lots of hidden humor in it. Because I'm treating a religious subject people think it can't be funny. Particularly Protestants."

Mr. Waugh smiled a little like a devout but contented cleric. "I think most of your writers nowadays lose all their delight in the material. I think it's something in the soul—a message they have to deliver. Words should be an intense pleasure just as leather should be to a shoemaker. If there isn't that pleasure for a writer maybe he ought to be a philosopher. A writer has no right to be like Lawrence or Hemingway, thinking they're prophets."

This reporter left Mr. Waugh but not before he took away with him a kind of rhyme—which pretty much went: "Evelyn, Oh Evelyn, you're good enough to be a sin."

November 19, 1950

FRANCES PARKINSON KEYES

IN RECENT writing experience, perhaps no author has had such phenomenal success as Frances Parkinson Keyes (rhymes with "sighs"). She has just come out with *Joy Street,* which, from all legible signs, looks like it will do better than *Dinner at Antoine's* (1948), which did better than *Came a Cavalier* (1947), which in turn did better than *The River Road* (1945) —each of which, by the way, successively cracked the million-copy mark. The golden touch, you'd say, and you'd be right.

And yet Mrs. Keyes doesn't know how to write a best seller. "Perhaps a clever author," she says, "much cleverer than I am, could deliberately set out to write a best seller and do it. He may be able to do it once, but I don't think he could go on doing it." And, for evidence, she cites her past three novels, saying: "If you were writing in a pattern, I don't think you could be that successful all three, and maybe four, times."

Not only does Mrs. Keyes not know how to write a best seller, she isn't primarily interested in the phenomenon. She is more pleased by the fact that she was chosen the outstanding Catholic woman in the United States for 1946. And, as for writing, she says, perhaps startlingly: "I have always been much more interested in being a woman of letters than a best-seller author. I want still to turn out the kind of work I have always been interested in turning out—biography and travel sketches and verse."

Mrs. Keyes was born in 1885, hard by the University of Virginia. At nineteen, she married Henry Wilder Keyes, the former Governor of New Hampshire and a United States Senator. Before Mr. Keyes died in 1938, his wife was already well on her way to becoming more famous than her husband.

When recently Mrs. Keyes' visitor entered her rooms, she rose from her chair with slight but nevertheless visible effort. "I am sensitive neither to age nor weight," she said. "I was not ever thus. I was for twenty-five years done up in an iron frame because of a minor spinal difficulty—a fall that was never X-rayed. I explain it to you, but I neither apologize nor do I wish to emphasize it. If you watch me get up or sit down you will see that I do it with my hands."

So considerately did Mrs. Keyes get her visitor over any difficulties he may have felt. The pursuit of information, nevertheless, was still on the agenda. How did Mrs. Keyes get started on a book? Had, for instance, *Dinner at Antoine's* gotten crystallized by some incident at a dinner party?

"Yes, it did," Mrs. Keyes said. "But it is impossible to generalize. Sometimes it is an impression, very often it is a real experience. Sometimes I pull various things together. An anecdote here, an experience there, an environment remembered— many things having nothing to do with each other begin to assemble and fall together. I begin to write and the people come alive and do what they please."

Didn't Mrs. Keyes think she ought to exercise more control? "If they don't come alive for me," Mrs. Keyes replied, "they won't come alive for someone else. As a matter of fact, it gets quite extreme. I have had cases where someone insists on staying alive even though I had planned his death."

But didn't Mrs. Keyes believe in enforced interment? "No,"

Mrs. Keyes replied. "I wouldn't change it. I think it would be dishonest writing if I'd do otherwise."

The author considered the entire question of honesty and best sellers. "You know," she said after a short while, "I am not a reviewer's author. I rarely get a good press. But I think you have to have a renewed feeling of reality each time you write, and the people must seem real to you, and you must put into each book the best you are capable of doing. If you don't, people are going to know it."

Technically, how did Mrs. Keyes make certain she was putting into each book the best of herself? "It's an extraordinary experience for me," Mrs. Keyes said. "I draft everything in longhand and read it aloud, making changes along the way. This version gets into triple space manuscript, and that's changed about forty times, and finally it gets into double space and I hope that's the end."

That seemed a fair enough safeguard. Was there any other test Mrs. Keyes applied to her effort to be honest? Mrs. Keyes nodded. "A solemn pledge I made to myself," she said, "that I'd never let anything leave my hands that didn't represent the most sincere and earnest effort of which I am capable. At that time," she added.

"At that time," Mrs. Keyes continued, "because I look back at the early things I did and I wonder how they got published."

December 10, 1950

CONRAD AIKEN

~~

JUST before Conrad Aiken went down to the fair if besieged town of Washington, where he was to take over the poetry chair in the Library of Congress, two friendly events occurred: a book of his, *The Short Stories of Conrad Aiken*, was published, and he paid a brief visit to this newspaper. As to the latter, only one problem presented itself: it was to find a place of privacy, which is a dilemma in any realm of the fourth estate. When one was found, its décor, delicate and pastel, conveyed an incongruous note in relation to Mr. Aiken's generously compact frame, strong, firmly-made head, and ruddy complexion.

Mr. Aiken did not mind. As a matter of fact, nothing of that sort could affect him, it appeared; obviously, Mr. Aiken struck a nice balance between sensitivity and matter-of-factness, between possessing culture and dispossessing it, and a room was a room and not an assault on the senses. Mr. Aiken, most famous as a poet, had published his first volume of verses in 1916, when he was twenty-seven; and so one wondered when he had been last engaged in the short story.

In 1934, Mr. Aiken said quietly, and the collection's name was *Among the Lost People*. He looked up. "It's from Mr. Dante," he said. "I remember during the days when T. S. Eliot worked at Lloyd's bank and I went to lunch with him quite often. He'd be reading small volumes of Dante—it was his lunchtime reading. I was already indoctrinated, though."

In Dante? Mr. Aiken nodded. "It was through Santayana. He gave a wonderful course in it, which later became part of his book, *Three Poets* [the three poets Mr. Santayana wrote on were Lucretius, Dante and Goethe], one of the great books of our time. In it Santayana makes out a case for the philosophical poet as against the fragmentary. Santayana was wonderfully witty, too."

Mr. Aiken's face did actually take on a glow of pleasure. "I remember," he said, "the time Santayana invited six people, myself included, to a seminar on Shelley. We'd have tea on each occasion and we read aloud the entire works of Shelley; it was a fine thing. Do you remember a poet by the name of Anna Hempstead Branch? She had something of a vogue around 1910, and I was very much taken with her. I loaned a volume of Miss Branch to Santayana. After reading it, he handed it back to me and said, 'Here is your Miss Twig.' "

Mr. Aiken had done a great deal of living in England, or hadn't he? "I moved there in 1921," he said. "First to London, then to Sussex. I bought a house in Rye, and which I had up until three years ago. I didn't stay all the time; I went and came." Mr. Aiken had done a London Letter for *The New Yorker?* "Yes," Mr. Aiken said, "under the name of Samuel Jeake, Jr. That was the name of the original owner of my English house. He was a philosopher and mathematician, and he invented an airplane which he launched off the town walls of Rye, somewhere around the 1680's. It didn't fly, of course," Mr. Aiken said with a touch of sadness.

"It was a wonderful house," he reminisced. "The walls were about this thick [Mr. Aiken demonstrated the dimension with his hands, about four feet it was], of stone, brick and tile. It took a plumber three days to cut through. It was supposed to be haunted, and I really had trouble selling it. One of the first applicants, I remember, wanted to be assured, and said if it is the least bit haunted, then it had to be amiably haunted."

Did Mr. Aiken think it was haunted? Mr. Aiken replied by indirection. "Do you know Malcolm Lowry?" The author of a very brilliant novel, *Under the Volcano?* The same Mr. Lowry, it turned out to be. "Lowry had been a pupil of mine," Mr. Aiken continued. "He'd come over and stay once in a while. One night he swore he heard high up in the house slow typing. Said he was convinced old Jeake was learning the touch system on the Remington typewriter."

Did Mr. Aiken care to declare himself on American letters? "Mr. Faulkner," Mr. Aiken said, "is the great American genius, the only adult writer of fiction we've had in the last twenty years on a major scale. *The Sound and the Fury* is a perfect symphony. And the so-called rococo in Faulkner, even when it becomes almost intolerable, is valuable as a part of that complexity of form, that density that texture must have."

Mr. Aiken, whose *Collected Poems* will be published next year, stood up to leave. He said, "You know the last time I came to *The Times?* I went to see Joyce Kilmer. I was trembling like a leaf. I remember glancing down at his typewriter and I noticed he was writing about Edgar Lee Master's *Spoon River.*"

December 24, 1950

E. E. CUMMINGS

~~

It is entirely within the realm of possibility that poetry is making a comeback. Or, to put it another way, maybe America is making a comeback. For look: Within this harassing one-year span we are on the eve of leaving forever, three of America's most experimental, most substantial, most gifted versifiers have won distinguished honors. Wallace Stevens took the Bollingen Award; William Carlos Williams the National Book Award; and now the fifty-six-year-old Edward Estlin Cummings has won the Academy of American Poets' $5,000 fellowship.

The thing to do, this writer reasoned, was to drop in on Mr. Cummings and offer him congratulations; and more, to check on the state of Mr. Cummings' heart and mind. Mr. Cummings, as always, was himself—which meant his heart and mind were as uncluttered as his frame was spare, his speech as exact and unembellished as his finely wrought, bony and ascetic face.

When you say the name Cummings, what generally comes to mind? For most of us it is the *enfant terrible* look of a Cummings poem on the page, the lower-case face of the type, and so on—which is tribute indeed to an experiment, a belief, rather, but which is not the entire story at all. What has been omitted are many pertinences. For example, that the poet is a painter, and that he has written masterful prose (*The Enormous Room* and *Eimi*), that he is a playwright (*Him, Santa Claus*), and, for still another thing, that he shows, in his newest verse, an even greater power than before. (Here are the last lines, the couplet of one of Mr. Cummings' most recent sonnets:—*do lovers love? why then to heaven with hell/Whatever sages say and fools, all's well.*)

After having dropped in on Mr. Cummings (some time ago), the second thing to do was to talk about poetry. Why did Mr. Cummings turn his back on the conventional upper-and-lower-case system and employ nearly exclusively the lower-case letter? "Sure, I'll tell you," Mr. Cummings said, serenely and simply. "Sam Ward, a New Hampshire farmer and a dear friend of mine, used to write to me. I remember once he wrote: 'we had a Big snow.' He'd write 'i' not 'I'—because I wasn't important to him. I got letters and letters from him. It is the most natural way. Sam Ward's way is the only way. Instead of it being artificial and affected, it is the conventional way that is artificial and affected. I am not a scholar but I believe only in English is the 'I' capitalized."

A Cummings poem always did have a modest look on the page, as well as holding a curious and challenging excitement. Mr. Cummings had believed in and stuck to his idea and now what had once seemed so alien *was* beginning to look more natural. Mr. Cummings, thinking on the question of belief, said, as he wandered about his room: "Pound once wrote a magnificent thing. 'What matters is not the idea a man holds, but the depth at which he holds it.'

"The only way I can define art is in a negative way; a poem is something that can't be translated. To define a thing is to limit it and a poem is infinite. I'll tell you what else I believe: the importance of intensity in art, which is what Pound was saying. I'd say 90 per cent of the human race believes in extensity, believes that two readers make a poem better than one reader, and that a hundred readers make it still better. And all that palaver has nothing to do with art. It isn't just one plus one plus one. A poem, a painting, lives in itself."

Mr. Cummings marshaled his arguments. "A man who lives intensely really lives, but a man who lives to be a hundred and twenty doesn't necessarily live at all. You say, 'I lived a whole lifetime in a moment'—a cliché that's true, and, vice versa, one takes a long train ride and it's a stinking bore. You read detective stories to kill time. If time were any good why kill it?

"Today so-called writers are completely unaware of the thing which makes art what it is. You can call it nobility or spirituality, but I should call it intensity. Sordid is the opposite. People don't have this luminous quality. Shakespeare is never sordid."

What writer dealt with the sordid? "Dostoevsky dealt with it from beginning to end. But, then, he had that luminous quality and transcended it."

Who was the least sordid writer? "Shakespeare," Mr. Cummings said, "because his poetry was the most intense. Take the Prospero lines in *The Tempest: To do me business in the veins of the earth/ When they are baked with frost.* Words," Mr. Cummings pursued, "which in prose would be nonsense. But these lines happen to be poetry and the greatest poetry."

They're wonderful lines—it's better than Hemingway.

"They're even better than O'Hara," said Mr. Cummings.

December 31, 1950

JAMES NORMAN HALL

✌

Not so long ago a sixty-three-year-old Iowan (Grinnell College, class of 1910) paid us a visit. His name, James Norman Hall; and he had just come from Tahiti because his newest book, *The Far Lands*, called for some sort of celebration. He had a bit of a time writing it. His close friend and collaborator, Charles Nordhoff, had died suddenly (that was in 1947), and for a long time after Mr. Hall says he felt stymied. Obviously, he came out of it all right because The Literary Guild snapped the novel up.

When you see Mr. Hall you're glad of any breaks he gets. Maybe he doesn't need them, but you're glad anyway. Without his trying to be, he's a winning fellow. He's tall, almost six feet, and painfully thin (maybe 145, soaking wet); his face is lean, leathery, but not lapidary; it is guileless and friendly, really. He looks in good shape, is sort of an unbrazen advertisement for living in Tahiti, which Mr. Hall has done pretty steadily now for thirty years. His conversation, after long pauses, is accomplished at a rapid clip, as though the talk were sprung from him, and this is accompanied by outward thrusts of his hands in deaconlike gestures. The effect is one hell of a thing: the average human being confronted by him may feel, without feeling ab-

normal, warm, friendly, sad, protective, loving (but not concluding).

Why had Mr. Hall gone off to Tahiti? If anyone knew Mr.
Hall's history during World War I it wasn't a very smart question. He had really been through the mill: British Army in
1914, machine-gunner in France, 1915, honorably discharged,
re-enlisted in French Army, became flyer in Escadrille Lafayette,
wounded, 1917, hospitalized, returned to United States Air
Service, rank of captain and flight commander to 94th Pursuit
Squadron, shot down inside German lines and prisoner from
May 7, 1918, to end of war. Well, the answer to why he had
gone to Tahiti was easy, wasn't it?

Still the question had to be asked, and Mr. Hall replied with a
simple gravity, "Because I like islands." Then he added, arm
shooting out: "Say, let me tell you a funny thing. I was sitting
in a restaurant with a completely strange man. (His street
wasn't my street.) I ordered clam chowder and the fellow
ordered fish chowder and we got into talk. When he heard about
my having just come from Tahiti, he said he came from an
island, too. What one? I asked. And he said, Oh, Manhattan."

The harmony of Mr. Hall's collaboration with Mr. Nordhoff
had been practically a household word. Had there been *any*
difficulty? "Yes," Mr. Hall answered. "I think the main thing
was, say, in something like wanting to get a guy out of a room.
Nordhoff wanted to get him out very meticulously." What
about himself? "Oh, I— I just wanted to get him out. You just
put him out. The reader knows he's walked out. You don't have
to tell the reader. That's where we had real trouble."

Did Mr. Hall have real trouble with any of the visitors to his
island? "No," he said, "only I do get a bellyful of people who
come out and don't speak the language and talk of patterns of
behavior and patterns of this and that. Nobody else bothers me,

particularly the natives. They know I'm a writer but they don't care. Chaplin came out and no one bothered with him either."

That must have been fine for Chaplin. Did Mr. Hall admire the comic artist? Mr. Hall did. Did Mr. Hall hold with Al Capp's thesis that the basis of humor was man's inhumanity to man, which he applied to Chaplin as well? Mr. Hall was wonderfully wide-eyed. "Now," he said, not with pugnacity but with awe and wonder, "I'd like to meet that man. I just don't believe that. I'd like to meet that man and talk to him and find out what Mr. Capp is about."

Having been a flier, did Mr. Hall think anyone had written well of that world? "Yes," he said, "I think Exupéry did flying the best of all writers, and Anne Lindbergh maybe was second best." Had he read any of Faulkner's stories dealing with aviators and their pathetic flying machines—"crates," Faulkner called them. No, Mr. Hall had not read them, hadn't known Faulkner wrote about planes.

Had Mr. Hall been having himself a time in New York? "I like to pop in on New York," he replied, "and maybe my best fun is to sit at my hotel window in the Commodore and watch the people go into the Chrysler Building and get into their offices and sit down at their desks and stay there until they leave again." Mr. Hall clacked his tongue and shook his head in a sort of puzzled admiration. "But I guess it's part of the world," he said. "It's really quite a show."

January 14, 1951

JOYCE CARY

JOYCE CARY, whose trilogy (*Herself Surprised, To Be a Pilgrim* and *The Horse's Mouth*) came out in England between 1941–1944 and proved a thumping literary success over here during the past few years, has been having himself a time on his first visit to the States. He's been lecturing and visiting and plane-ing and training, and always on the go with no respite. He's been enjoying it. "I like it a lot," he says. "There's been a lot of good talk." When you say—thinking that Mr. Cary has passed his sixty-second birthday—well, take it easy, anyway, he answers: "Yes, but I'm tough, y'know, pretty tough."

So be it, "tough" Gully Jimson Joyce Cary. You want him to be tough because you want him to write another book, and another after that. He is, as a matter of fact, writing one now, called, beautifully, *Prisoner of Grace*. Said Mr. Cary, "It's giving me a terrible time." How far was Mr. Cary in it? Mr. Cary couldn't say because Mr. Cary doesn't work from left to right. "I work every day," he explained, "but at different parts of the book. Quite early in the book I get my last chapter taped. And several of the big scenes. I have to know if they'll do."

That, obviously, was a fascinating, if unorthodox, method. "I'm always working at a book," Mr. Cary continued. "I have a little davenport beside my table and it's got a few drawers in it, and I have notes for two other books in there. When I get an idea I write it down and put it into one of the two drawers. It's very restful from the book I'm working on."

He paused just long enough to manifest some concern lest he be considered too frivolous. "The reason why it is possible for me to do that," he said, "is that all my ideas are part of the same system. I'm continually getting impressions, usually of a character in a situation, and I generally get it down as a sketch, with a little monologue or dialogue and some description. I have hundreds of them put away in the davenport drawers."

Mr. Cary's speech isn't noticeably British, but his clothes are: baggy, loose-fitting, ancient, permanent tweeds. His well-knit figure gives the impression of his looking younger than his age, though his bony face, ascetic, gentle and durable, is ageless. Thinking of age, it was nice to know that Mr. Cary had published his first novel, *Aissa Saved*, when he was forty-three. "Ah, yes," Mr. Cary said abstractedly, "my main trouble was my Trinity schooling. The political and philosophical foundations of my learning made me want to be sure my books weren't phony and that they added up.

"My friends," Mr. Cary explained, "were philosophic and I had to measure up to that. I knew when my ideas were invalid or my judgments superficial. My education was largely by talk, and then I went rushing off to the Balkan War in 1912. Why? . . . Because we didn't think there would be any more wars. (It was a nice little war.) We didn't believe the Kaiser would go to war. The interesting thing is that we saw what was true: that it would be the ruin of Germany."

All this, then, the early carefulness, the rushing off, gave Mr. Cary a late start. "Yes. And I destroyed so much." What were the influences on Mr. Cary—was it Russian? "Do you know Aksakov?" Mr. Cary asked. "His *A Russian Gentleman? Years of Childhood?* You see, there is in them a completely fresh, open atmosphere. Aksakov stands beside the stream: he's no terrific nationalist, there's little violence." Then was Aksakov like Turgenev? "The tone is a bit like *Sportsman's Sketches*. But it would mislead you to say he is like Turgenev. He is like himself. The Russians and Conrad had a great influence on me. Otherwise I wouldn't know."

What about Mr. Cary's painting? (He had been a painter.) "I haven't time," Mr. Cary said. "One doesn't have time for two arts. Though I wouldn't have given up my three years in art school. I see a great deal—I think from training. My eye records. It's very funny. People tell me I'm going to meet a beautiful gal and when I meet her all I see is a complexion. I can paint her at forty. I see her bones and I know how ugly she is going to be. People don't use their eyes. They never see a bird, they see a sparrow. They never see a tree, they see a birch. They see concepts. I mean writers, too."

Mr. Cary looked squintingly at his interlocutor. He said: "Art has to give you a kick in the belly. Look here, I read three months ago Hemingway's *The Killers*. That's a perfect job; not merely a technical success. What's unforgettable is that last glimpse of Ole Andreson waiting to go out to get murdered. Right off Hemingway has broken the crust. He's got you, he's got you hooked and you can't get off. I know that's a masterpiece because it gave me a permanent kick in the belly."

February 18, 1951

NOEL COWARD

As every past generation's schoolboy knows, Noel Coward can't help but go on being bright as Clifton Webb, dapper as Jimmy Walker, slim as a jack-knife and productive as General Motors. Here today and gone tomorrow (back to Jamaica), Mr. Coward paused briefly in this metropolis to celebrate the advent of another of his books—short stories this time, called *Star Quality*—to record on a four-side LP his *Conversation Piece*, and to assure his publishers he will definitely complete the second part of his autobiography, already titled *Future Indefinite* (first part: *Present Indicative*).

When this reporter sat down with Mr. Coward in his rooms at a midtown hotel, Mr. Coward clasped his hands on his lap and stared amiably. "Go ahead, Mr. Coward," this reporter (who wasn't bringing any coals to Newcastle) said, "Go ahead and talk." Mr. Coward demurred. "You shoot," he said.

Well—casting vaguely about—are you going to go on television? "I loathe television," Mr. Coward said, not quite answering the question. He stood up. "The first time I watched television—oh, Lord! The faces began to fade out, they smeared away." Mr. Coward acted out the business of a face smearing away.

Jimmy Durante had, however, said about television, "That

box has got to get you. You going to have to march right into that box." "Ah, Jimmy Durante," Mr. Coward exclaimed, "I love Jimmy." Mr. Coward did a bit of monologue that was pretty fair Jimmy Durante. Then he said: "Oughtn't we to get bookish?" (There is no record of how both hands reacted to this tentative question.)

There is the record that the conversation piece did turn, at least momentarily. How did Mr. Coward accumulate a book of short stories? "Oh, I do one and put it in a drawer. I do a spurt of them. And then the end in sight prompts me to write a few more in order to have a book." How was the autobiography going? "Absolutely limping. Some of it is so witty and then—it isn't."

Mr. Coward managed to get a good deal of work done. Aside from short stories, autobiographies, verse ("Not poetry," he said), musicals, movies, music, recordings, acting, he had written some forty-five plays. "The legend of my playboyishness," Mr. Coward said, "has lasted into my vintage. If the legend were true, how could I have managed to get anything done?" How did Mr. Coward manage? "I get up at 6," Mr. Coward said, "I start work at 7 and work four and a half hours, and I *still* get to the beach before lunch. The thing is to have time, and peace."

The only man who is as versatile as Jean Cocteau thought for a minute, or seemed to be thinking for a minute, about time and peace. "Maugham has the whole thing taped," he said after a bit. "I think he has a routine of working seven hours a day." Did work go easily for Mr. Coward? "With the plays," Mr. Coward said, manifesting not a moment's hesitation.

"With a play I go straight on until I'm finished. I do it straight on the typewriter. It was five days for *Blithe Spirit*. No, no changes. It was all complete. Maybe a few typographical errors. The quicker I write my plays, the better they are. I know this is a dangerous fact for would-be writers."

But would-be writers weren't Mr. Coward's concern. "What I adore," Mr. Coward said, "is this supreme professionalism. I hate more bitterly than anything an unprofessional job in a profession. I'm bored by writers who can only write when it is raining."

How did Mr. Coward feel about his acting? "Ah," he said, "one of my finest bits was in 1939 when I got myself into Russia without a diplomatic visa. That was wonderful. I got in by sheer acting. They kept me four hours at the frontier. It was my medicine case—you know, aspirin and pills and all that—it threw them into a frenzy. I had to pantomime it, and that went down like a dinner. I had to do it four times and I had them in the aisles. There were spies everywhere. The spying was the worst, really terrifying. I was never so thankful to get out of a country. I did make one complaint: I turned on the bath and a tadpole came out."

Would Mr. Coward say a little more about outstanding virtuoso performances? "Jolson at a benefit," Mr. Coward went on, "crouching down and singing to each individual. There are so few solo artists! Beatrice Lillie, Merman, Harry Tate—oh, he was one of the great solo artists. He always looked so permanently offended. Sid Field. Olivier in *Richard III*. Hayes as Queen Victoria. Alfred and Lynn in practically anything. Miss Bette Davis in *All About Eve*."

And what about Noel Coward in *The Scoundrel*?

Mr. Coward knitted his knitted brows. "I thought I was very good," he said, "in the parts I was dead."

February 25, 1951

CECIL WOODHAM-SMITH

THE author of *Florence Nightingale*, which was such a tremendous success in Albion and which may very well duplicate the distinction here, is a youthful-looking, white-haired English woman with a delicate, translucent skin and the very bluest of eyes. Mrs. Cecil Woodham-Smith, the author we have in mind, came here to correct the proofs of the American edition of her biography—and she had "a most laborious time." It was the various spellings that made for the difficulty. Mrs. Woodham-Smith was using *The New York Times* as a check on correct American spelling. Obviously, it had been a maddening helter-skelter search. The laboriousness came to an abrupt end one day when her husband said to her, with perhaps unforgivable simplicity, "Why don't you get a dictionary?"

It took Mrs. Woodham-Smith eight years to complete her book. The first years turned out to be a sorting and organizing job. ("It took ages," Mrs. Woodham-Smith said, "and I'm very slow.") There were masses of material (now at the British Museum): 113 packages of letters and documents, for example; other sundry and ill-assorted packages consisting of all sorts of memorabilia and trivia, a trunk with still more things thrown into them pell-mell.

"It was exactly like looking through a peep show," Mrs.

Woodham-Smith said, "and it is the greatest source of astonishment to me that readers liked this book. Those people, the Nightingales, kept everything—old bills and calendars. They couldn't bear to tear anything up, excellent creatures that they were. They all wrote madly and all expressed themselves. Now, for instance, in Miss Nightingale's later life she kept all instructions to the cook, and even the orders to the butcher. It was quite incredible. That will never happen to me again."

Mrs. Woodham-Smith had taken six years for the actual writing. Had she worked at it steadily? "When you get accustomed to working you get bad-tempered if you break it. I've been away from work a month now," she concluded sadly. Was she feeling bad-tempered? "Yes," Mrs. Woodham-Smith said. "What I deplore," she went on, "are the people who say why don't you write a novel. There's room for a woman who doesn't write a novel, don't you think so?"

One could only paraphrase Alice at the tea party and say, "There's *plenty* of place!" But that did raise the interesting question of fictional biography. Mrs. Woodham-Smith had rather firm ideas on the subject. "Fictional biography is to be deplored," she said. "If you say someone put his arm on the table and smiled, then you have to have a letter that says I saw him put his arm on the table and smile."

But supposing, one countered, you knew that the personage in question was both indolent and amiable? "Then," Mrs. Woodham-Smith re-countered, "you must say, 'He was in the habit of doing so.' You must, if you are an historian, put down evidence. The rest is not history." Did Mrs. Woodham-Smith believe that fictional biographers ought to write historical novels instead of novelistic histories? "Yes," Mrs. Woodham-Smith said unqualifiedly.

"An historian friend of mine once said," she said, "that one must use concrete nouns and active verbs. The quality of a book depends on it. I'm frightfully interested in style. I don't like the purple patch. I do like the style that goes on smoothly without arresting your attention by artificial means. It's such an infinite trouble and you don't get any marked effects."

Had Mrs. Woodham-Smith written in the past? "I have written really all my life," she answered. "Before I was married I wrote advertisements; after I was married I wrote on a free-lance basis, but still did some advertisements for an agency. Though really my interest has always been history, and all my life I read the nineteenth century. It never seemed as if I'd make any use of it."

What were people reading all through Mrs. Woodham-Smith's life? "The eighteenth century," she said. "They still are. You see, when I was a girl in England the influence of Lytton Strachey was very great. I remember him saying to me: 'Very few books in the world are worth reading, and most of them are French.' It was something of a revelation to discover the Victorians weren't dull and even pompous. And, of course, Florence Nightingale, who was born in 1820 and died in 1910, saw the whole Victorian panorama."

Mrs. Woodham-Smith paused, then apparently decided to say it. "But as far as I personally am concerned," she said, "what I fear really I am is just a bookworm. My melancholy conclusion is that I know no one, I've been nowhere, and I know nothing."

March 4, 1951

JAMES JONES

THE author of the tough, powerful, loving and—most critics agree—wonderful novel, *From Here to Eternity*, comes out of Robinson, Illinois, and is twenty-nine. Beyond the statistics, James Jones is youthful, earnest, spontaneous, honest, unembellished and spare. He retains his fighter's figure. He fought at 135, and he couldn't have put on much weight since. He has a prize fighter's relaxed poise, a sort of easygoing quality that, obviously, one mustn't take advantage of or misjudge.

How had Mr. Jones reacted to the sweepingly affirmative reaction of the American reading public? "It was kind of startling," Mr. Jones said. "I don't think I thought about it much. Maybe I had daydreams once, like Thomas Wolfe, about being a great writer. But that was phantasmal. I just felt relieved that the book was finished."

Could Mr. Jones elaborate on the feeling of relief? "Yes," Mr. Jones said with utmost amiability and candor. "I remember once driving in my jeep along the Freeway into Hollywood and saw blood on the road. There was always some sort of an auto accident along that road. And the thought struck me that even if I were to get killed I had at least gotten the book written. Finishing the book haunted me in the Army."

Mr. Jones had started writing *Eternity* in the Army? Mr. Jones had—in odd moments, in the evenings, on Saturday afternoons. "I had been writing for a number of years before that," Mr. Jones explained. "They were mostly stories, parts of two other novels that didn't come off. I didn't know beans. I was just learning. I read *Look Homeward, Angel* and it meant everything to me at that time."

Was that how Mr. Jones had come to Scribners? "Yes, there was that character of Max Perkins in it." Had Mr. Jones met Mr. Perkins? "Once, no, twice," Mr. Jones said. "The first time for an hour, the second time for a few minutes." Had the real Mr. Perkins jibed with the Wolfe portrait? Mr. Jones nodded affirmatively. "The talks went off fine," he said. "I was as high as a kite. I don't think there is any doubt that in his own field Perkins was a very great and creative man. He saw about two hundred pages of the book, which I later revised considerably."

Had Mr. Jones read a great deal in the Army? "Everything and anything I could lay hands on," Mr. Jones answered. "I read so much I don't even remember what they were. I idealized Wolfe at that time to the point of evolving a theory that Wolfe was revolutionizing the novel by getting around plot, which has a certain amount of artificiality. My idea now, though, is that the simpler you can keep your style and narrative the better off you are."

In the Army one could get away with reading, but could one get away with writing? Mr. Jones laughed a little. "I remember," he said, "I bought myself a portable which I kept in the barracks. One Saturday afternoon I had the typewriter sitting on its case on my bunk and I went off to the latrine. When I came back some guy had put a sign on it, 'Genius at Work.' I got a lot of kidding on that. I was kind of piqued at it."

Did Mr. Jones care to say anything about literature today, about his contemporaries? No, he didn't really. Apparently, though, Mr. Jones wanted to talk around it. "You know," he said, "I'm no intellectual, I'm no intellectual radical. But I'd always been a rebel. Now I think politics injure a writer. (I don't want to sound like I'm lecturing.) A writer should be able to be a Democrat or a Republican or an American radical. A writer should be everything. He should be able to be everybody. Do you know what I mean? I mean there is a good deal of pessimism around. That if the world were to be blown up I mean that I could even enjoy the spectacle—though I wouldn't be able to write about it."

There was laughter and unanimity on the last point. Mr. Jones had sold *From Here to Eternity* to Hollywood. Did he want to go out and pitch in? "Yes," he said, minus every complication that a writer might have about such an admission. "I'd like to go out and write the story for the movies. Though maybe I couldn't do it, I sure would love to cast it."

March 25, 1951

ARTHUR KOESTLER

No MAN is an island, said John Donne and Ernest Hemingway. It could have been said by Arthur Koestler. He has the contemporary need to be in touch with political and cultural life everywhere. "I would like to divide my time between this country and Europe," he says. "A political writer of our time can only hope to get a balanced picture of the world if he knows America not as a visitor but as a resident involved in everyday life. And the same goes for Europe. The hopelessly distorted and one-sided view which the European holds of America and the American of Europe is one of the main sources of the political and cultural confusion of our age."

Mr. Koestler (whose novel *The Age of Longing* is recently out) is economical in his behavior and *sec* in his thinking; he is also courteous and gentle, and above all he *listens* (which is rarer than you might think). And though he is partisan and passionate and you think of him as someone who has made an enormous spiritual investment, his mind has autonomy: the head ultimately rules the heart. Mr. Koestler, in this sense, can be said to be "disinterested."

Talking to Mr. Koestler is a fascinating experience. He really walks the floor—and the path he takes, somewhat unseeingly, is a devious one that courses its way among a variety of appointments; the pacing is more or less in time with the thinking, and the thinking is astonishingly brisk. Nevertheless this particular meeting unfolded without a mishap.

Had Mr. Koestler's present extended stay altered his view in any way? "The longer I live here the more bewildered I get with the literary life," Mr. Koestler said. "I don't mean the writers. You have, all in all, a greater number of first-rate novelists here than there is anywhere else. What disturbs me is something different. Let me put it this way. If you were to ask me what a writer's ambition should be, I would answer with a formula: to trade a hundred contemporary readers for ten readers in ten years and for one reader in a hundred years."

Did Mr. Koestler mean that we had our literary eyes focused on the hundred readers? Mr. Koestler meant that. "However much innate integrity the writer has," he said, "publishers, reviewers and editors focus his attention—consciously or unconsciously—on immediate success here and now. In America the social climate has made the creation of art into an essentially competitive business."

Mr. Koestler stepped neatly about the room then stopped abruptly. "I know of a young American writer who once headed the best-seller list and is now paralyzed and on the verge of a nervous breakdown because of the fear that if he doesn't repeat his success he will be regarded as a passé novelist. And this very excellent young writer is still under thirty. Can you fathom the whole horror of what this implies?"

But isn't English and European literature equally competitive? "Not by miles," Mr. Koestler said. "There are no best-seller charts; circulation figures are not made public; publishers' ads are only a little influenced by sales; the lists have an equality for all the current authors; circulation of a book is largely independent of campaigns, supermarket stunts, public relations and so on. And the best-seller chart is the symptom."

Wasn't this difference rooted in the difference in the social structure? "Yes, of course," Mr. Koestler replied. "Your competitive society could not help but influence literary life. It would not be possible and perhaps not even desirable to induce American publishers to imitate conservative British and European publishing. But it is up to your own writers and organizations like the Authors League to protect the integrity of their art by drawing a line between what is indispensable commercially and what is grotesque and altogether excessive. I imagine it would have an extremely healthy effect if those American writers who have figured on best-seller lists and cannot be suspected of sour grapes would sign a demand for abolishing what is excessively commercial and grotesque. But there is much in American literary life that I admire."

It would be most interesting to know what they were—Mr. Koestler might see with a fresh eye what was under our very noses and therefore invisible.

"The required reading of modern authors at your universities is extremely interesting and healthy. The earnestness, and sometimes even passion, with which criticism is given and taken shows remarkable seriousness. The personal relations between editor and writer." Mr. Koestler concluded his ticking off. "All this," he said, "is really admirable and does not exist in Europe."

April 1, 1951

HELEN MacINNES AND
GILBERT HIGHET

YOU could call the Highets—as a certain intellectual but frivolous lady did—the Lunts of Literature. It is a notion not to be
pursued, though admittedly it makes a point. Miss MacInnes is
as attractive as Lynn Fontanne, and Mr. Highet as handsome as
Alfred Lunt. They've been together pretty continuously, too:
they were born in Scotland, met at Glasgow University ("I met
this bloke the first week at the university," Miss MacInnes says),
were married in 1932 and have stayed married since. They arrived in the States in 1937 (Mr. Highet was changing over
from Oxford to Columbia). Except for a time when Mr. Highet
was a liaison officer during the recent war, they've been here
and together, even working in the same room, but separately, of
course. *The Art of Teaching* was Mr. Highet's newest book, and
Neither Five Nor Three, Miss MacInnes'.

They think they complement each other. Mr. Highet's background of classicism is perpetually enlightening to his wife.
Miss MacInnes' interest in the novel and her apparently effec-
tive way of getting Mr. Highet to read fiction has given a human
and esthetic edge to her husband's scholarship. Mr. Highet has
been working on a book on Juvenal for fifteen years and his
wife has become an expert on that prophetic writer and his
times; on the other hand, Miss MacInnes is directly responsible

for Mr. Highet's vast acquaintanceship with *War and Peace*.

Mr. Highet plans to finish the Juvenal within the next half year. "Juvenal was way ahead of his time," he said. And Miss MacInnes said, "Did you know that he was the originator of many of the expressions we think are out of Shakespeare or Homer? It was Juvenal who first came up with 'bread and circuses' and with 'strong body, strong mind.' "

What about Miss MacInnes, what was she up to? "I'm going to see the country on Gilbert's sabbatical," Miss MacInnes said. "We're going to New Orleans and to Jackson, Mississippi, where Gilbert is lecturing." Wasn't Jackson, Mississippi, Faulkner country? "Yes," Mr. Highet said, "we might go near the master's outer wall. Maybe look up the Snopeses." And then what? "We're flying to Scotland to see our parents and then fly right back to California," Miss MacInnes said. "I've never been West. I'm going to see all that country."

Mr. Highet was going to see all that country, too. But he was also going to be finishing his Juvenal, and that was what his mind's eye at that moment was focused on. "I'm damn well going to check every word with pencil ticks," he said in a determined tone. "No mistakes in this one."

Miss MacInnes turned back to the question of work. "I never know quite when a book starts," she said. "I don't worry about it too much. I don't believe in forcing the pace. I take it when I can, sort of seize the moment. We get a lot done in the evenings. ["No telephones," Mr. Highet said grimly.] That suits Gilbert. He doesn't feel he has continuously to entertain me. He doesn't have to say, 'Darling, what about going to the theatre? What about going to the opera tonight?' " Mr. Highet tossed in apologetically, "Not that we stay in all the time." Miss MacInnes, it must be said, smiled back at him benignly.

"The fact of the matter is," Miss MacInnes said, "Gilbert reads all the time. Even when he's putting on his socks he's got a book propped up on the table." Were they translations from the Greek? Mr. Highet laughed. "We've got to get rid of the 'thous' and the inversions. How are you going to explain these things to students? They read some clumsy and archaic passage and they want to know why that's so. I couldn't even read the Russians because of the awful translations."

"But Gilbert once read all of Proust," Miss MacInnes said. "The reason I knew Helen was going to be Mrs. Highet," Mr. Highet said, "was during our courtship when I had read Proust. It must have been dreadful. I analyzed everyone's motives continuously. Helen took it very well, and I knew then she was the woman."

April 8, 1951

J. B. PRIESTLEY

THE man many critics compare with Charles Dickens stared at
his visitor with enormous wide-awake eyes though he had only
gotten up. Stockily made, robust, J. B. Priestley (whose newest
novel, *Festival,* was recently published) gave the impression of
making a fine breakfast companion. He looked cheerful and he
sounded uncomplicated—two requisites that this writer insists
on from any acquaintance with whom he would share his boiled
eggs and first coffees.

Mr. Priestley had come here on his most protracted holiday
ever. He felt he had earned it. "The novel," he said, "is much
bigger than I had planned. It expanded very naturally—I think
simply because the people came to life. It got bigger and bigger,
I worked harder and harder, and it got later and later. There
were other deadlines I had to make besides. I found myself need-
ing a complete break. I decided to kill two birds with one stone;
it was important for me to keep in touch with America and to
have a holiday as well."

Mr. Priestley lifted himself out of his comfortable chair. "It's
rather an ironical thing," he said, "but I used to be known
before the war as a man who didn't like America, notwithstand-
ing the fact that I brought my family of nine out to Arizona.

Any man who pays fare for nine people from England to Arizona must like the country."

Mr. Priestley's previous novel, *Bright Day*, had been written some four years ago. It had done extremely well in England but hadn't here. Why was that? "I don't know why," Mr. Priestley replied. "The whole point interests me. I think certain books succeed here because they are written in a certain mood and answer certain needs. I have been reading James Jones' novel. I think it is a real novel, that he's a real novelist. But this is what's astonishing: here's the best-paid, best-dressed army, and before there's any fighting. Yet all the men are in frustration and despair. One would have thought they were pretty well off."

Mr. Priestley's eyes narrowed a bit. "It would be interesting," he said, "to compare those soldiers to Kipling's soldiers baking under an Indian sun. But there is a fixed mood of self-pity— apparently it answers some need in the critic today. And I think conversely that people like myself who don't write from that particular mood and who are not violent and angry tend to get underrated. After all, there's no reason why self-pity and violence should be the permanent theme of literature. Chaucer didn't write that way. Shakespeare didn't, except for one or two things. Fielding and Goldsmith didn't either. I think of myself as eighteenth century: writers wrote everything then, essays, novels, plays, there was a variety, a professionalism."

Did Mr. Priestley feel that this literary phenomenon of violence was of very recent vintage? "It's been happening in the last thirty years," Mr. Priestley replied with leisurely equanimity. "The assumption is held among many critics that art is synonymous with introversion. The formula would go: introverts produce art, extroverts produce entertainment. One quality is looked for—intensity. That, again, is nonsense. It is only a passing fashion, this attempt to get intensity at all costs."

Was anyone writing in America today who Mr. Priestley

thought was unfashionably good? "I'd like to pay tribute to one novelist," Mr. Priestley replied after a thoughtful pause. "James Gould Cozzens," he said. "I personally like him. I don't mean the others aren't novelists. But to me Cozzens is free of that tortured quality and on the other hand he has that broad, objective quality I like so much."

Yet there hadn't been much criticism around Mr. Cozzens. "The critics," Mr. Priestley said, "nevertheless pay a good deal of attention to contemporary literature here, far more than criticism gives it in England. I once suggested to the book trade that they find a thousand or two thousand pounds in order to subsidize one or two first-class critics. The thing, though, is simply that you can't reduce a novel to a sonata. That's the trouble with criticism. It wants to turn fiction into a pure art form which gets you to say that Flaubert is greater than Balzac, and Henry James greater than Tolstoy. It just isn't so. I was once a critic myself, you know, but there's nothing like writing a novel that sells a great many copies to make people think you're not to be taken seriously as a critic."

Then, to sum up, Mr. Priestley didn't think the literature of violence was the whole story? "I don't like the literature of the mutilated," Mr. Priestley said. "I call it compensation literature. Why can't literature come out of an excess of energies and zest and love of living? I don't denounce the other, but I say meekly and humbly it is not the whole of literature."

April 22, 1951

FRANK YERBY

EVERY once in a while—not often, mind you—there appears on the literary horizon an author who, for one reason or another, can't help but produce best-selling novels. Frances Parkinson Keyes is one such. Frank Yerby is another. Now, take Frank Yerby: at the ripe age of not quite thirty-five, he has come up with his sixth novel, *A Woman Called Fancy*, and the chances are very good (as good, say, as Ray Robinson beating Jake La-Motta in a rematch) that it will be a thumping best seller, as were the five novels before it. Each of the five were book-club selections and each had a distribution of at least a million copies. *The Foxes of Harrow*, Mr. Yerby's first, went to over two million.

The phenomenal Mr. Yerby was born in Augusta, Georgia, a town he lived in pretty steadily for his first twenty years. He went to school in Augusta's Paine College, to Fisk, to the University of Chicago. "I was a fairly dreadful kind of student," Mr. Yerby says. "Nonathletic, very studious, took scholastic honors, what the boys today would call a grind. I had my master's at twenty-one, and I could have had my doctorate at twenty-three if I hadn't run out of money. Which," Mr. Yerby sagely addended, "is all to the good."

How did Mr. Yerby write a novel? "I've done a novel every

year for six years," Mr. Yerby said. That meant, then, quite a tight regimen, didn't it? Mr. Yerby nodded. "I frequently write right around the clock," he said. "I work as much as eighteen hours a day. Not only that; I rewrite. I rewrote *Fancy* three times. And not only that: I do a lot of research. I read, read, read for my preliminary work. I've been spending as much as six hours a day in the library on background material for my new novel."

Mr. Yerby didn't exactly hesitate. He said, "My notes for a novel always outweigh in bulk the novel itself. Sometimes it's three times over." Well, this data struck an observer as all to the good; at least, one could feel, Mr. Yerby's novels weren't "quickies." It turned out that Mr. Yerby had pretty strong feelings on the entire matter of the relationship between writer and reader.

"I think the novelist," Mr. Yerby said, "has a professional obligation to please his reading public." At the age of twenty, when Mr. Yerby was writing poetry for the little magazines, was he writing for any other reason than that he had to? Or wasn't that it? Of course that was it. "Because a writer has a duty to his reader," Mr. Yerby said with honest passion, "it doesn't mean in any way that he has the right to write *down* to his reader. All the brows, high, middle and low, should be able to read his book, but for different reasons. The novelist has no right whatsoever to insult his public."

If one took a hypothetical situation in which Mr. Yerby found his work lacked any corresponding response in the reading public, would he go on writing? "I would have to," Mr. Yerby said. "I write because I have to. What I get out of it financially doesn't come under consideration at all. I write exactly what I feel and think I want to do, but within that framework I try to give pleasure to the reading public. Take it from the other angle: the novelist hasn't any right to inflict on the public his private ideas on politics, religion or race. If he wants to preach he should go on the pulpit. I mean this from a professional, artistic point of view."

There would be many instances of accepted great novels that Mr. Yerby would have to combat. Mr. Yerby knew it. "Now, for example," he said, "when I read *Anna Karenina*, I find myself skipping the political, peasant-in-relation-to-the-land parts. I really feel Tolstoy was getting that sort of thing out of his system. That sort of thing just isn't the novelist's job."

What if you were a novelist interested in contemporary political life? "It's important to know," Mr. Yerby countered, "your character's emotional life, his emotional reaction to political ideas, but what the political ideas themselves are is a matter of indifference to the novelist. I hate above all things the heavy hand of the author off-stage creaking the on-stage machinery. The novelist must try to write with a universality of appeal so that it hits all segments of the people. To do that, a novel must have characters that are alive and a story that is interesting. It is my contention that a really great novel is made with a knife and not a pen. A novelist must have the intestinal fortitude to cut out even the most brilliant passage so long as it doesn't advance the story."

Did Mr. Yerby feel he had the intestinal fortitude? "I do," he said, "but not enough. The spirit is willing but the flesh is weak. I have learned though. My danger has always been a too great fluency. I used to be adjective-happy. Now I cut them with so much severity that I find I have to put a few adjectives back."

May 13, 1951

NORMAN MAILER

‿⁀

ON JANUARY 31, Norman Mailer noted the fact that he had become twenty-eight years old. "I was a young man in my prime," he said the other day with hardly any irony, "when I wrote *Naked and the Dead*. The army was the only milieu I ever had. It was like living in a society where rumor has the same validity as fact, like a tight community where you can weep about people you never saw. Like someone says, 'This guy got knocked off in a patrol.' And everyone feels bad."

If there is such an attribute as being restfully intense, Mr. Mailer has it. It is a quality of intensity that is without strain and makes no demands on a companion. Strangely, and comfortably let it be added, while Mr. Mailer's thought and speech have intensity, Mr. Mailer himself—beneath the mind and voice as it were—is perfectly relaxed. It is an attractive paradox that creates intellectual stimulation and physical relaxation simultaneously.

He said, "I wrote *Naked* in fifteen months. The new one, *Barbary Shore*, is half the size and took me three years. I don't think of myself as a realist," Mr. Mailer said after a pause, during which he obviously thought back to his first, and very impressive, novel. "That terrible word 'naturalism.' It was my literary heritage—the things I learned from Dos Passos and Farrell. I took naturally to it, that's the way one wrote a book.

But I really was off on a mystic kick. Actually—a funny thing—
the biggest influence on *Naked* was *Moby Dick*."

Had he known while writing it? Mr. Mailer nodded. "I was
sure everyone would know. I had Ahab in it, and I suppose the
mountain was Moby Dick. Of course, I also think the book will
stand or fall as a realistic novel.

"I may as well tell you what the title of the new book means,"
he said. "It has a double meaning. 'Barbary,' for me, is a very
rich word. One of the meanings is barbarism and the other, not
in the Oxford dictionary, has romantic connotations. You think
of the exotic, of pirates, of romantic things."

Were we coming back to romantic things? "I think the tendency as you come closer and closer to doom and disaster," Mr.
Mailer said, and stopped and began again. "There is a tendency,
given such a condition, to move closer and closer to amorous
wish fulfillments."

How did Mr. Mailer feel about being an author in an age
that was moving, as he put it, closer and closer to doom and
disaster? "It is probably one of the worst periods in history for
a writer," he said with hardly any hesitation. "To be a novelist
today is absolutely a bone-cracker. The knowledge that you are
embarking on a novel that may take ten years of your time is
vitiated by what you read each day in the newspapers. I mean if
you are trying to do work of the devotion of *Ulysses* or *Remem-
brance of Things Past* or *The Magic Mountain*. On top of that,
the fundamental problem of knowledge is involved."

Mr. Mailer stared fixedly at his companion. "In the past," he
said, "a novelist could create a world view, a whole thing in
itself. It is different today because knowledge is broken down,
departmentalized. Time and time again the novelist louses up
his work with jargons and special knowledge. And yet you can't
eschew it. It's better to fail that way than to ignore this condition and keep on in some little cubbyhole. If a writer really

wants to be serious he has to become intellectual, and yet nothing is harder. Intellectuality delivers the writer to self-questioning and to despair at his own limitations; it vitiates the attempt at large, serious works because you are unable to suspend the critical faculties even at the times when you should."

Eliot once said perhaps the main difference between the good and bad poet was not so much one of talent as it was the inability of the bad poet to be *unconscious* at the right times. Mr. Mailer nodded at least in partial assent. "I'm beginning to have a pride in writers. They are radical, always disturbing. What they write has nothing to do with what they profess, which is usually silly.

"A great writer always goes to the root, he is always coming up with the contradictions, the impasses, the insoluble dilemmas of the particular time he lives in. The result is not to cement society but to question it and destroy it. Faulkner may profess all sorts of things, he may even be off on a white-supremacy binge, but actually the total of his work has caught the horror at the same time that it has caught the fact that he loves it. A great writer has to be capable of knowing the rot, and he has to be able to strip it down to the stink, but he also has to love that rot. A writer has to have a tough mind, the toughest mind of his time. And he has to have a great heart."

June 3, 1951

MALCOLM COWLEY

WHETHER for or against, it would be folly to deny the dialectical leap backward so many readers and writers have taken. The Twenties are with us, perhaps, like the world, too much with us. But they are with us none the less. The most recent revival concerns a single book, *Exile's Return*, an account of that era by Malcolm Cowley. Now, as the chronicler of the golden age of modern American fiction, affection and bravado, Mr. Cowley is the horse's mouth. And we went right to it.

"The purpose of the revision," the fifty-three-year-old, handsome Mr. Cowley said, "was partly to bring out the story. The book is really a story. I saw after seventeen years where I'd failed to bring out the structure. The whole European adventure was sort of a fairy story with the son running away from the cruel stepmother and wanting to look for treasure and coming home to dig for it, and possibly finding it, in his own father's backyard."

Now, one knew that Mr. Cowley composed a brilliant book of verse, *Blue Juniata*, and he had written five years later, in 1934, *Exile's Return*. But what about the book in between that Mr. Cowley was supposed to have written—*The Lost Generation?* Mr. Cowley's smile was gioconda. "This book, *The Lost Generation*, doesn't exist," he said. "That was an early title for what turned out to be *Exile's Return* and some reference books picked it up. It is nice to be the author of a nonexistent book because it is the cause of no embarrassment. Furthermore, critics have written that *Exile's Return* is an improvement over *Lost Generation*. It's the lost book of the lost generation," Mr. Cowley summed up.

What did Mr. Cowley think when he went over his book? "What impressed me going back seventeen years," he said, "was what a damned good time we had. Scene after scene comes to mind of everybody laughing and shouting and what not. In those days you never imagined that parties could be doleful and that people would be thinking about their souls."

Was it because people were more innocent then? "I suppose they were," Mr. Cowley said, merely politely. "It started out because there was an enormous store of vitality from the war that ended so soon. All the emotions that weren't expended in combat—that was the beginning and then one got in the habit of working hard and then having a rousing party. I suppose it *was* innocent. I remember one party where I was playing hide-and-seek with a bunch of Dadaists."

Mr. Cowley was silent for a moment. "One of my fantasies," he said, "is to think of the literary scene as a stock exchange of writers. A characteristic in this country is the marked fluctuation of authors' reputations. If a writer gets a great deal of praise, it doesn't take a keen-eyed prophet to tell that within five years his stock will have sunk far below par. And if any author of talent is completely neglected as Fitzgerald was for fifteen years, then you can bet with a good chance of winning your money that his stock will jump up to 500 or 600 on the exchange. After a while you become cynical about the prevailing quotations. You judge a writer by what he is worth and you risk your status on the bet that some day his stock will be back at par."

What was Mr. Cowley doing for the Fifties? "I'm doing a new edition of *Tender Is the Night*," Mr. Cowley replied. "Did you know that two years before his death, Fitz rearranged the whole novel, making a chronological story of it?" Was it better that way? "It's a much better version. Although it gives a less brilliant introduction, it gives a much sounder novel. You get the full force of Diver's ambition at the beginning and the full force of his failure at the end. That's what I'm doing—following out Fitz' rearrangements and correcting the spelling. Fitz was the worst speller who ever failed to graduate from Princeton."

After Fitzgerald, what? "I'd like to do for the Thirties what I did for the Twenties," Mr. Cowley said. "The Thirties are becoming the unknown era. The real climax of the Twenties was 1930. The end of the era was not the stock-market crash. I put the discovery into my revision of *Exiles*. It was New Year's Eve, 1930–1931.

"All during 1930 people thought the depression was temporary. It was just a matter of waiting it out. If you lost your job, your wife went out and bought a new dress. But at the end of 1930 you knew it was to be a long pull, and business men reduced their staffs by 50 per cent and then the new era suddenly started. So that gave me an end to the book—and that's where you might say I want to pick up to write the story of the 1930's.

"And that era ended on August 24, 1939, with the signing of the Russo-German pact."

July 8, 1951

RAY BRADBURY

THERE is this genre, getting quite a play these days, known as science fiction. Well, one of its leading luminaries came to town the other day—in the ordinary way, let it be said at once, and not in a space ship or a zodiacal zeppelin—and it seemed a good idea to ask him a few questions. Ray Bradbury, the author of, most recently, *The Martian Chronicles,* took to it all right. He liked being asked questions, and he liked answering them, too. He's a young fellow, having broken out of his shell in 1920 in Waukegan, Illinois; and he's a pretty big fellow, looking more like football material than like interplanetary stuff.

First off, before defining the field, how did Mr. Bradbury come to be writing science fiction? "I'm not only a science-fiction writer," Mr. Bradbury replied. "I started out as a straight writer. Now I work in three schools, you might say, simultaneously: one is small-town life, one is science fiction, and one is straight fantasy."

What was the difference between science fiction and fantasy? "Science fiction," Mr. Bradbury said, "is really sociological studies of the future, things that the writer believes are going to happen by putting two and two together."

And making not only four but five? "I've just finished a story I call 'The Pedestrian,'" Mr. Bradbury said illustratively.

"There's a traffic problem now and it's possible that some years hence the pedestrian will be outlawed. I have a fellow taking a walk one night and a traffic car eases up alongside him. There are robots in this police car and one of them asks the pedestrian what he's up to. I'm taking a walk, he says. Why, the robot asks. To breathe some air, the fellow answers. But you've got an air conditioner, the robot says. I wanted to see things, the fellow says. But you've got a television set, the robot says. Anyway, the pedestrian gets taken off to an insane asylum."

That was pretty grim. What was fantasy? "It's the improbable," Mr. Bradbury said, thereby implying a slogan, "Pedestrians beware!" It was difficult to recognize the improbable these days. What was it? "Oh, if you had a leprechaun or a dinosaur appearing in the streets of New York—that's highly improbable. Science fiction is a logical or mathematical projection of reality."

Did Mr. Bradbury think, really, that some good writing was being done in the field? "I'm afraid," Mr. Bradbury said, "that as in any literary form there are only a few people who are trying to do something really good. In science fiction there are the space operas, a Western in space; you herd rockets instead of cattle. But there are some science-fiction writers who are trying to think in human terms of real human problems. The form has a bad name because of the space operas. You say science fiction and people think of Buck Rogers and Flash Gordon."

Mr. Bradbury, of course, wasn't writing space operas. As a matter of fact, his straight stories made the O. Henry collection twice and *The Best American Short Stories of 1946*. It was logical, then, to ask Mr. Bradbury who his influences were. These were, it turned out, Anderson, Hemingway, Steinbeck and Cather. "Between the ages of six and ten," Mr. Bradbury said, "an aunt of mine read Poe to me, and I read the Tarzan and Oz books. But I stopped reading fantasy when I began to write because I wanted to bring back to science fiction something fresh and new. It needed revivifying because it was contemplating its own navel."

And Mr. Bradbury felt the way to do it was by introducing human concerns and values into its ray-ridden spaces? "The field can only come of age when good writers can influence it," Mr. Bradbury said with conviction. "The mechanical age is crushing people. People are confused. There is too sure a knowledge that God isn't there when you put your hand out. When we move out into space, what a revolution!"

Revolution? *There* was a nettlesome word. But what sort of revolution? "Supposing there are people out there," Mr. Bradbury said. "How will this jibe with Christianity or Judaism? Supposing there was no original sin? No Adam and Eve? Do they have a soul? Suppose in Mars a creature looks like a dog but is twice as intelligent as a man? These religions will have to do some quick stepping."

One supposed that we'd do the usual missionary work. "Yes, we might," Mr. Bradbury said. "We might just close our eyes to all the differences and convert the heathen Martian. We'd probably say it was another case of God's wonders."

At any rate, it was something to think about for somebody, this problem of the Marsmen and God. Mr. Bradbury shook hands when he left. He just left, walked out, sort of ambling. No momentous blinding take-off or anything like that.

August 5, 1951

PHYLLIS McGINLEY

ANYONE who reads poetry these days—and we are not so many that we can go about boasting in iambic pentameters, let alone in heroic couplets—ought to be familiar with Phyllis McGinley's beautifully manipulated, unostentatious, first-class versification. For those who are not, there is currently in circulation the lady's most recent exemplar, a volume of verse titled *A Short Walk From the Station*. For those of us who do not know the lady but know only the elegance and urbanity of the poetry, there is something of a biographical surprise about her. Miss McGinley was born in, of all the places, Ontario, State of Oregon.

It was Oregon, Nebraska, Colorado, Utah—that sort of country. "I was brought up in the real Wild West," Miss McGinley related, "when the cowboys came in and threw their horses' reins over the hitching posts and instead of Sunday baseball games we had bucking bronco contests. I used to ride to school three miles on a pony, where sometimes my brother and I were the only pupils, and where sometimes there was no teacher. Actually we were anomalies. My father was a land speculator and the family was always moving around, and maybe that's why those roots in a suburb mean a lot to me. I fell in love with trees. There weren't any out there—a few cottonwoods up by the irrigation ditch and that was about all."

Well, to leap across the ditch, did Miss McGinley write what is known as *light* verse? "Yes," Miss McGinley said, "most of it is." Now, that "most of it"—that was important in what it omitted. Did Miss McGinley have in mind some of the poems she wrote—they were appearing more and more frequently—that touched and moved the reader? "The line between light verse and poetry is very thin," Miss McGinley replied, and thereupon bravely embarked on a subject that was difficult indeed. "In fact," Miss McGinley went on, "the line is practically not there at all. I think, though, I've arrived at a distinction: the appeal of light verse is to the intellect and the appeal of serious verse is to the emotions. That's the only way I can tell one from the other."

The popular notion that light verse made one laugh wasn't true then? Miss McGinley believed it wasn't. "People don't always laugh at light verse; certainly they don't always laugh at wit. I remember a Suckling poem—though I don't remember the line exactly: 'How could she dance so lightly with such a marble heart.' The whole thing turns on wit, but you don't laugh at it. You enjoy it intellectually. The primary impact of light verse is intellectual; it's the only criterion I can arrive at— and that's why Pope is the great exemplar of light verse. Even the appeal of Herrick and Lovelace is more to wit than to the emotions."

What about Auden? A contemporary had said he was the greatest intellectual poet since Pope. "Only at times," Miss McGinley said. "There is a great deal of emotional impact in Auden. Pope seems all intellect. There is no intoxication in Pope, but there is great satisfaction. Do you know why Auden has been compared to Pope? He helped revive Pope. But they aren't really alike."

Listening to Miss McGinley, hearing her speak with a certain verve, yet experiencing a deeply quiet quality in her, made the writer wonder hwo to describe her. Tranquillity wasn't quite right; it implied something passive. It was more the sense of a woman who had perhaps resolved those deep conflicts that keep most of us hopping, skipping and jumping, and had thereby gained repose. Miss McGinley, then, let it be construed, has repose, an inner calm, an inward order.

Completely oblivious to such private divagations, Miss Mc-Ginley pursued her theme. "Marvell, of course," she said, "Marvell's *To His Coy Mistress*—there is the perfect example of light verse that is great poetry." But wasn't one emotionally moved by Marvell? "In lines," Miss McGinley partially agreed. "There are lines that move you, like 'But at my back I always hear.' The over-all impact, however, is intellectual delight."

Miss McGinley didn't exactly shift gears. "A light-verse writer is a kind of critic. A critic's stock-in-trade is his ability to be angry at injustice, stupidity and pompousness. But today the critic and light-verse writer find it increasingly difficult to express social anger. The whole world is angry. All of us are deflated. In times of ease it is the duty of such a writer to deflate, but in times of unrest and fear it is perhaps his duty to cele-brate, to single out some of the values we can cherish, to talk about some of the few warm things we know in a cold world."

December 9, 1951

CHRISTOPHER ISHERWOOD

AT FORTY-SEVEN, Christopher Isherwood has had enough dramatic triumphs in fiction and literary triumphs in drama to have kept him from getting excessively excited over John Van Druten's dramatization of his short novel, *Goodby to Berlin*. He did admit a bit of excitement because, even though once removed, his name was on Broadway for the first time. What was more interesting to him—and it is the kind of double thing, or coincidence, that Mr. Isherwood looks for—was the fact that *The Dog Beneath the Skin* (a collaboration with W. H. Auden) was opening in Cambridge in the same week. Mr. Isherwood, boyish-looking and thoughtful-looking both, permitted himself a minute on the Van Druten play, called *I Am a Camera*.

"The title," he said, "is taken from the opening words of the book, and I say it about myself." Mr. Isherwood then focused away from himself: "He's sitting in the window," said Mr. Isherwood about himself, "and he says, 'I am a camera, quite passive, only recording.' At that particular moment he's not turning his experiences into an art form, he's simply collecting them. At the end of the play (it was a line I wrote for the play), he, the main character, says, 'The camera has taken all its photographs and now it is going away to develop them.' The play was entirely conceived and written by Van Druten, but I did have a chance to say my opinion of it later. He's a very old friend of mine and has known the book for a long time."

Aside from *The Dog Beneath the Skin,* what were the other plays Mr. Isherwood had written? "*The Ascent of F-6* and *On the Frontier.* They were all collaborations with Auden. *On the Frontier* was a flop; it was a play about Hitler. It was the best play technically, the one in which we really learned about the theatre, and because we learned thoroughly it was less irresponsible. The irresponsibility contributed a certain charm to the others, but this one was too reasonable, perhaps too sensible."

One wondered if getting even this refracted, oblique taste of Broadway gave Mr. Isherwood a keener desire to write for it. Mr. Isherwood demurred instantaneously. "My real interest is entirely in writing novels," he said. "If I wanted to write a play it would be a verse play and it would be with Auden. Though," Mr. Isherwood added in afterthought, as though getting a play on Broadway would be one way of doing it, "it's wonderful to come to New York and see one's friends."

Mr. Isherwood had settled in California since how long? "I've been there since 1939, on and off. I've been a U. S. citizen, you know, for the past five years. I'm just about off to England and Germany. I'll be in England for Christmas. I'll also get to Italy." Mr. Isherwood's face expressed undiluted and unmeasurable delight. "I've been to every country in Europe except Italy (and Switzerland and Norway). I've always reserved Italy. Imagine at my age having a country reserved. And Venice is really one of the places in my mythology" [Mr. Isherwood said my-thology].

Had Mr. Isherwood read Hemingway's novel and had he liked Hemingway's Venice? "Oh yes," Mr. Isherwood said. "I liked the Venice part of the book tremendously."

Mr. Isherwood's last books had been a small and first-class novel, *Prater Violet,* and a first-class book on South America,

The Condor and the Cow, a travel book that read like a novel. What was Mr. Isherwood working on right now?

Mr. Isherwood thought a bit, then apparently made up his mind. "I'm working on a novel now," he said. "I'll tell you the title—it's one that isn't known yet: 'The World in the Evening.' It's about America. No," Mr. Isherwood admonished himself, "it's *set* in America, let's be accurate.

"I've written a great deal on it," he said. "I've been writing it since 1947. Then I suddenly discovered it was two novels. One was the Christopher Isherwood type, the 'I' telling the story. The other is the one I'm working on. It's in the first person, but the chief character is not me."

What about the other novel, the Christopher Isherwood one, was that going to get done? "Oh sure," Mr. Isherwood said, "as a matter of fact, it's a novelette and belongs in a volume with *Prater Violet* and another novelette." What other novelette? "I know all about that one too—it's about Greece."

It was nice to know so completely about the work not quite yet in progress. Mr. Isherwood agreed. "But *you* know something, too. That I'm working on a novel—and the title. That's the news," he said, "that's the only news." And Mr. Isherwood vanished, next to be seen in London, Berlin and Venice.

December 16, 1951

VAN WYCK BROOKS

A SMALL but significant anniversary has just come up for Van Wyck Brooks: twenty years ago exactly he embarked on his extensive and intensive and impressive literary history. Now, with the publication of the fifth volume, *The Confident Years: 1885-1915*, Mr. Brooks is done with his masterwork—which bears the over-all title *Makers and Finders: A History of the Writer in America, 1800-1915*. Twenty years, a song goes, is a very long time. But one gets the idea, after being around Mr. Brooks, that it wasn't—that it was, on the contrary, fun. Mr. Brooks is by way of celebrating his sixty-fifth year this year, too; a youngish age when you consider that he's been a controversially famous critic ever since 1915.

Why 1915? That was the time Mr. Brooks' first really controversial work, called *America's Coming of Age*, had its coming-out. This writer remembered it well (not in 1915 though); it had opened several literary doors for him and had taken him to the heart of certain critical problems, and he said as much. Mr. Brooks, sporting unmatched tweeds and a corduroy waistcoat and his familiar white mustaches, shook his head ever so impersonally. Considerate, gentle and disarming, and reminder that Mr. Brooks is of the genteel tradition, he nevertheless revealed a touch of iron. "It isn't right," he said with finality.

"The book was right for then but not for now. It wouldn't hit the nail on the head now."

Makers and Finders ended at 1915. Why not a more contemporary finale? "No," Mr. Brooks said, "I'm not going on beyond that. It ends with the first war. Why? First of all, it's difficult to write a history of the contemporary scene, and in the second place you have to get the stuff behind the writer, you have to get the social history of the times and you have to get perspective. So you can't do it. At least," Mr. Brooks amended, "*I* can't."

Mr. Brooks, guessing what was perhaps obvious in his interrogator's mind, took the offensive. "I began with 1800 because it was the year Jefferson became President. Something happened in that year, something that could be called American. The Jeffersonian view of life or of human nature, a world outlook which had a generous, global character, has been the keynote of American writing. You can call it democratic liberalism. Most of the serious writers did follow that line."

Mr. Brooks gazed around the "talk" room of the newspaper and smiled—benignly it seemed—at the Miro on the wall. "I had a lot of reasons for writing the history," he continued after a while. "As a matter of fact, I'm working on a book explaining those reasons—it's called 'The Writer in America.'" Was Mr. Brooks writing it right now? He was. Didn't Mr. Brooks take any sort of a rest? He laughed. "I like to work," he said, "at this kind of work."

Would Mr. Brooks anticipate his new book and speak a little of the reasons behind the history? "I suppose," Mr. Brooks said, "the idea was to create a literary memory. Everybody is so isolated in this country—you know, the famous talk of America being lonely. The country is so big, everyone is so scattered, there are so many kinds of people and races, and I wanted to create the feeling that a great deal has been done in a much more unified way than has been thought of."

Did Mr. Brooks merely want to, or did he find it so? "Obviously, it's there," he said. "Almost anybody writing now can find somebody in the past like himself, and can share the feeling that he is not isolated, that he has a connection which is what the Europeans have—and this is tremendously reassuring and stimulating. Then I wanted to bring together all the sections of America. The South hates New England and the West hates the East. Well, I wanted to show there is a much closer relationship between these sections than was realized, that we weren't so provincial, and that we *were* influenced. Melville and Whitman began as imitators of Irving, just as Farrell followed Dreiser. The instinct of emulation is very powerful."

The instinct got weakened sometimes, didn't it? "One of the worst things," Mr. Brooks said, "is the writer who attaches himself to a wrong influence. Anderson attached himself to Lawrence. Sherwood was a folk writer; Lawrence led him astray, and it is one of the reasons why Sherwood's novels never really made the grade. Hart Crane was Whitmanesque and also an admirer of Rimbaud who hated everything Whitman stood for; it confused Crane."

Just about an hour after Mr. Brooks made the above series of statements he remarked, having completed a bit of a tour of this newspaper, how cheerful the people he met seemed to be. What he failed to recognize was their instinct of emulation: aside from other causes, a main cause was Mr. Brooks himself. His natural cheer cheered them up, one after the other.

January 13, 1952

JEAN STAFFORD

~

AT THE age of twenty-eight Jean Stafford came out with her
first novel, *Boston Adventure,* and in so doing walked through
the door marked literature with almost alarming suddenness.
That was 1944. Miss Stafford started on it in 1940; during
some of those four years she was on the staff of *The Southern
Review.* Almost three years later, in 1947, she published her
very different novel, *The Mountain Lion,* and the fact that it
was different did not diminish her promise or her stature. Her
third novel, *The Catherine Wheel,* is just out, and it is now
apparent if it wasn't before that Miss Stafford is positively here
to stay.

"Beauty," the poet says, "is momentary in the mind." Perhaps it is, but one comes away from a meeting with Miss Stafford thinking for longer than a moment that the lady has beauty
—in the structure of the face, in the muted manner of speaking,
in the aura of sentience that surrounds her. One might have just
sat—it wasn't an easy thing to begin (just how?—just what?),
and so one just did begin—routinely.

"I was born in California," Miss Stafford said cooperatively,
"and grew up in Colorado. After college I went to Germany for
about a year. I don't know why. Then I taught at Stevens College in Missouri. It was a course called Communications and

consisted of two days of writing and a third day of conversation. Then I got to Boston."

Was Miss Stafford writing all this while? When had she started? "I started writing," Miss Stafford said, "as soon as I could write, which was at six. I wrote a poem, a brilliant poem, when I was six." Miss Stafford recited it:

> *Gravel, gravel on the ground,*
> *Lying there so safe and sound.*
> *Why is it you look so dead?*
> *Is it because you have no head?*

Had the six-year-old Miss Stafford's passion for writing shocked her parents? "Oh, heavens, no," Miss Stafford exclaimed softly. "My father was a writer of Western stories under the name of Jack Wonder and he wrote stories with titles like 'The Transmogrified Calf'—so that I certainly didn't shock him. I wrote a long story when I was about eight, called 'The Unsuccessful Amateur,' about kidnapping. In all my stories I was a man about thirty years old."

Had Miss Stafford's father influenced her? "There was a strong Western influence," she said. "I also read the dictionary from the time I could read. My language was incredible. I remember in one of my stories writing that a man had *oleaginous* black hair. I somehow managed to get hold of a Smith Premier typewriter; it had eight banks and looked like an organ. That was when I was about eleven."

Did Miss Stafford agree with the critics who were struck by the marked differences between her first two books? Miss Stafford did. "They were entirely different books, those two. There wasn't any basic change in me; the material was so different in each and required different treatment. What I would like eventually to do is to fuse the two manners."

An attempt at defining briefly the two manners was in order.

Would Miss Stafford give it a try? Miss Stafford thought, quite briefly considering, and then went ahead. "The first one is leisurely," she said, "a good deal more embroidered. It's contemplative." She hesitated, then said, quite decisively, "I think *Boston Adventure* is old-fashioned; it's filled with digressions, for example. *The Mountain Lion* is a more symbolic book. The symbols are apparent, though I didn't know what they meant at the time I wrote."

Often critics demanded that an author be conscious of every bit of what was being written. Miss Stafford shook her head. "It's sad that one loses a state of innocence. Novels written with too much consciousness, of psychoanalysis say, is one of the troubles today."

There seemed to be a dialectic at work: innocence, consciousness, an innocent consciousness, or a conscious innocence. "You have to get back to the innocence," Miss Stafford said. "Not only that. You need to get back to even the confusions you had, which all help. I think the self-consciousness today, the over-editing, is a mistake. They say Dickens needed an editor; if he had had one he wouldn't have existed. Dostoevsky and Melville are good examples of that. They wouldn't have existed either."

Then Miss Stafford thought overcarefulness was a major flaw today? Perhaps Miss Stafford only half agreed. "The writer today is competent," she said. "The English writer can't write a bad sentence, but too often it doesn't add up. Writers have been directing their talents to tiny things. There's a fear of making a mistake, of sticking your neck out, there is a finicking. There are so many writers who aren't writers. Now, I don't mean bad writers. There are a lot of bad writers whom you wouldn't give house room to, who nevertheless are real writers."

January 20, 1952

MARY ROBERTS RINEHART

TO HAVE passed your seventy-fifth birthday and to be erect and alert and gracious is something of an achievement. To have achieved all that and written a new book to boot is a triumph. And so one defers to Mary Roberts Rinehart——

"You are not going to call me the queen of them all, are you?" Mrs. Rinehart started right in. Mrs. Rinehart's guest guiltily shook his head. "I hate to be called that," she said. "It gives me the pip. It isn't true and it's—it's ridiculous."

Mrs. Rinehart studied the situation. "The extent of my audience pleases me, though," she said after a while. "It ranges from Gertrude Stein to stevedores. My chauffeur was once waiting for me down at the waterfront. Some stevedores were hanging around a fire and my chauffeur went up to get warm. Who do you drive for? one of them asked. He said Mrs. Rinehart, and the stevedore said, I've read all her books. *The Wall* was the best one she ever wrote. I wish he'd say it about my new novel, *The Swimming Pool*, but that's too new, isn't it?"

How did Mrs. Rinehart know Gertrude Stein had been a fan? "That's what Alice Toklas wrote me," Mrs. Rinehart replied. Did Mrs. Rinehart get a lot of mail? "My mail is wonderful," she said. "It is affectionate and sweet and is a joy and a burden, because I answer every letter I get. Saturday is mail day. I devote all day Saturday dictating and I sign every letter myself. Each one has something different to say, so you couldn't have a form letter even if you wanted one. It's a constant surprise, though, that people want to read me; I'm always terrified at each book."

What was the frequency of terror undergone by Mrs. Rinehart? "Counting some omnibus books, this is my sixty-first," Mrs. Rinehart answered, neither proudly nor humbly. "I've written every kind of thing. I've done politics, travel, war correspondence, movies."

And, of course, the novels and the detective stories, the plays and the Tish stories.

Mrs. Rinehart waggled a bit. "I've never written a detective story in my life." Would Mrs. Rinehart kindly explain that? "I'm not primarily interested in clues," she explained. "I'm primarily interested in people and their motivations. When the crime story began to be interested in people it began to grow up. My contribution was *The Circular Staircase,* which came out in 1908; it was supposed to have helped the crime story grow up." Was that her first crime book? "It was my first book of any sort," she said.

Thinking it out and putting two and two together, Mrs. Rinehart had averaged over a book a year (not counting omnibuses) for over forty years. That sounded as if it took considerable dedication and discipline. "There is frightful discipline," Mrs. Rinehart assented strongly. "Writing is the hardest work in the world. When I'm working I lead a very disciplined life."

Did Mrs. Rinehart manage to keep up on her reading? "I'm extremely catholic in my reading," she answered at once. "I read fiction and nonfiction. There on my table," Mrs. Rinehart pointed to a haphazard pile of half a dozen shiny looking books, "is Marquand's new novel, *The Blessing, The Cruel Sea* and Herbert Hoover's memoirs. [Mrs. Rinehart's guest reached out to Mr. Hoover's book, opened it and noticed the inscription:

"With thirty years of continuous esteem," signed Herbert Hoover.] I'm an incessant reader," Mrs. Rinehart pronounced with some finality.

How did she feel about writing today? Was it different from her early years? Was there any observable change? "Well," Mrs. Rinehart said, "just looking over the field, I'd say it was much easier for the writer when I began. The new author is up against 5,000 to 6,000 new books each year. The life of the average novel is shorter now because of the quantity of novels brought out, and the magazines are taking less fiction. That's a drastic change. Fiction used to be the—the vehicle—that's the word— to carry the advertising. Today the world is so full of interesting events and people and discoveries that the article has moved forward and fiction has moved back."

Mrs. Rinehart qualified: "That's just as I sit back and think about it." She then did sit back and, perhaps in a kind of sympathy with the young writer, said wearily, "I would hate to start out today, quite frankly. I would really hate it."

February 3, 1952

DYLAN THOMAS

IN 1950 THE brilliant, aseptic Welsh poet Dylan Thomas (Dylan rhymes with penicillin) visited us for the first time. He is back a second time now—to read his own and other poets' verses at the Ninety-second Street Y.M.H.A., the Modern Museum and scores of colleges and universities—as much by popular demand as by his own wish. In celebration of this event, New Directions is bringing out his new poems, *In Country Sleep,* and in celebration of a more personal sort this writer engaged Mr. Thomas in a repeat performance talk. Though Mr. Thomas—it was an absolutely reliable bet—wouldn't repeat himself, couldn't repeat himself. And so, inexorably, it turned out.

In the course of the first talk (May 14, 1950), Mr. Thomas described himself as "thirty-five years older, small, slim, dark, intelligent, and darting-doting-dotting-eyed." He then added, "Say I am balding and toothlessing. I am also well-dressed." Mr. Thomas wasn't slim then, and still isn't; he is still fair, with plenty of unruly hair, enough teeth, and his eyes are round and sleepy-looking. His tweeds are definitely unpressed. Mr. Thomas, as a matter of fact, could easily have stood in for Heywood Broun on the occasion when he was described as resembling an unmade bed. Mr. Thomas, it is nice to be able to report, continues all in all to remain intelligent, imaginative and unreconstructed.

The talk at first was on poetry in general and Thomas Hardy in particular, who turned out to be Mr. Thomas' favorite poet of the century. But Mr. Thomas was also a prose writer of talent, and one wondered how he thought about the two mediums. Did he, for example, care less and less about prose? "No," Mr. Thomas said, "as you grow older they are more and more separate in what you feel. When you are young you are liable to write this bastard thing, a prose-poetry. When you get a bit older you find they get separated, and prose becomes more clean and spare."

One felt that about Eliot's prose. Mr. Thomas nodded. "Eliot does keep them separate. He writes beautiful prose—only because it's nothing to do with the verse. A poet can't write extravagant prose: it would be a slopover. A prose writer can write extravagant poetry. Joyce is the direct reverse. He wrote simple, clean poetry and marvelously imaginative prose. With most people it's the opposite. Writers should keep their opinions for their prose."

Supposing, the interviewer said, you were not you and I were not I——

"I'd believe it," Mr. Thomas said succinctly.

And then not-I asked not-you, why shouldn't poets have opinions in their poetry?

"Opinions," Mr. Thomas proceeded, "are the result of self-argument and as most people can't argue with anybody and especially with themselves, opinions are bloody awful. There are opinions, of course. In dramatic poetry for one, but most of us are lyric poets. It was Eliot in this century who showed that one could talk about any subject in verse, except one's self."

Then wasn't there some sort of discrepancy in what Mr. Thomas was saying? "I suppose," Mr. Thomas said, "the thing about opinion should be qualified." That was precisely what Mr. Thomas had been doing, hadn't he? "The slant," Mr. Thomas went on, "the tilt of the mind informs the poetry."

Mr. Thomas kept his Between-the-Acts little cigar in the corner of his mouth, his head tilted at an angle away from the smoke. "I like to put down the word 'blood.' It's a curious kind of word; it means insanity, among other meanings. It's part of the tilt of my mind that I put it down often."

Mr. Thomas and his guest drank. "What is interesting," he pursued, after a while, "is the way in which certain words either lost their meaning or their goodness. The word 'honor,' for instance. A world fit for heroes. A world fit for Neros is more like it."

Why did words lose their meaning or goodness? "The wrong people crowed about them," Mr. Thomas said, looking like an owl.

How long was he going to be here? "About three months," Mr. Thomas said. "It will be my last visit for some time. I will have had the universities and they will have had me."

The writer wasn't taking that statement seriously at all.

"Well," Mr. Thomas said, "*I* am."

Would he sum up?

"Poetry," Mr. Thomas summed up, avoiding what might have sounded theatrical, "poetry. I like to think of it as statements made on the way to the grave."

February 17, 1952

TRUMAN CAPOTE

ONE crisp noontime this writer was walking in a most unlikely neighborhood and came upon Truman Capote. "What're you doing around here?" he asked Mr. Capote. "Oh, I'm going to have lunch with the Olivers," replied the twenty-seven-year-old author. "Who under earth's heaven are the Olivers?" "You know," Mr. Capote answered, dealing his words quite slowly, "Sir Laurence and Vivian."

That's one thing about Truman Capote—his affection for pronouncing his friends' names a bit differently. The other thing about him—that is, that one notices right off—is that he looks a little like a toy. That's what some people *say*, anyway. If he is a toy, he nevertheless has a mind that would turn those big thinking cybernetic machines green with envy. As a matter of fact, his mind has enough good steel in it to turn too many human beings the same violent color—and it has, no doubt about it. Mr. Capote's appearance is lamblike but all intellectual bullies are warned not to be deceived.

Though there are indications of description above, this writer thought it the better part of valor to have Mr. Capote describe himself. Mr. Capote, in his turn, thought it an amusing game. "Well," he said in that deceptively innocent voice, "I'm about as tall as a shotgun—and just as noisy. I think I have rather heated eyes." What on heaven's earth were heated eyes? "I don't quite know," he laughed, "but I didn't mean it complimentary." Mr. Capote worried the problem. "Let's see," he said. "I have a very sassy voice. I like my nose but you can't see it because I wear these thick glasses. If you looked at my face from both sides you'd see they were completely different. [Mr. Capote demonstrated.] It's sort of a changeling face."

Well, that sort of did it, didn't it? Mr. Capote offered a footnote. "Do you want to know the real reason why I push my hair down on my forehead? Because I have two cowlicks. If I didn't push my hair forward it would make me look as though I had two feathery horns."

What about writing now? Mr. Capote was the author of four books, the most recent *The Grass Harp*, which was already in rehearsal as a Broadway play. How had Mr. Capote found the task of transposing the novel into drama? "You don't transpose," Mr. Capote said decisively and, as it turned out, illuminatively. "Playwriting has very little to do with literary talent. The theatre is so extraordinarily visual, and in order to write for it I had to forget the novel. It's as though someone asked you to take a painting and make a statue of it. It's impossible. You can make the statue carry the same feeling and motivation as the painting, but it's a totally different thing. I actually looked at my book twice."

Mr. Capote's work had been unusually controversial. How did he look at criticism? "I think it's very seldom that criticism is pertinent. The point for a writer is to have somebody help him. That's hard for anybody to do, even for the critic. The most fortunate thing for a writer is to get criticism that helps him."

Was there something in criticism that Mr. Capote liked or disliked *personally?* "I've had some very decent things written about me. That doesn't mean I liked them best. What I personally dislike is when critics refer to my work as fantasy. I don't mean to attack fantasy; it's really one of the most difficult things to do. I just don't write it, that's all. I'm trying to do something that's psychologically and emotionally true. If it is true, it just isn't fantasy." Who was writing fantasy? "Walter de la Mare," Mr. Capote said. "It's wonderfully good fantasy and it's terribly difficult to do well."

Now, to take a good jump, what about this problem of decadence in fiction today? "If what some young writers are writing today is decadence, then let's have more of it," Mr. Capote said stingingly. "I think what people mean is extravagance. Any extravagant imagination seems to run into this criticism. People imagine it's immoral. And immorality is related in people's minds to political issues. Perhaps fear of Russian propaganda is back of it. The Russians seize on this kind of thing. The perfect example is Gide. Until he disavowed communism the left press sang his praises. When he broke away, the left press turned on him like a pack of hornets and called him decadent. It has *nothing* to do with morality."

Mr. Capote faltered a little, out of earnestness rather than out of any lapse. "All writing," he said, "all art, is an act of faith. If one tries to contribute to human understanding, how can that be called decadent? It's like saying a declaration of love is an act of decadence. Any work of art, provided it springs from a sincere motivation to further understanding between people, is an act of faith and therefore is an act of love."

February 24, 1952

C. S. FORESTER

❦

RIDING up the elevator to meet C. S. Forester, one might have had a reasonably high expectancy that he was about to say hello to a celebrant—of the secular variety, of course. Mr. Forester had a brand-new Hornblower novel between boards, this time called *Captain Hornblower*. And the film *The African Queen*, based quite scrupulously on Mr. Forester's novel, was having a splendid life in the cinema houses. No celebrant, though, Mr. Forester. If anything, he looked glum and even forlorn.

He lit a cigarette, propped up a couple of pillows at the head of his bed and sprawled. It was discernible that the fifty-two-year-old Mr. Forester, though enveloped in a heavy bathrobe, was bony to a fineness.

"I have a funny, unprotected feeling," he started right in, thereby justifying first impressions. Mr. Forester looked off for a long, soft moment, then looked at his visitor for a swift, scrutinizing one. "It's the first time," he then said, "I haven't either a job or a book going in thirty years. It gives me a queer, unprotected feeling. I wonder about how my book is going to go. When you're putting down a thousand words every day, you don't care too much about the notices and the sales."

Why wasn't there a job? "I came to New York because of a job. There has been a good deal of publicity about it—that I was going to write a Navy history for television. Well, this week we mutually decided not to go on with it, the network and myself. So I'm out of a job before I had it."

Why wasn't there a book going? "I thought," Mr. Forester explained, "I'd be working on the Navy history. But I'm leaving New York and I'll start right in soon as I leave."

Was it always a thousand words? "One thousand words more or less is a fixed minimum. I find the actual writing a toilsome bore. The only way to get it done is to set your course for a given number of words every day. If tomorrow is just as good as today, then three weeks go by before you know it. You just have to go ahead each morning and get the miserable thing done."

Mr. Forester was still a British subject? "My sons are American," he replied. "One of them is in the navy and I give you three guesses what his nickname is." Was it Horatio? Mr. Forester looked a bit downcast. "Hornblower," he muttered. "I must say he has got a sensible idea about it, and laughs at it. I don't know why it is that writing a best seller makes you an object of contempt for the younger generation. My sons are all terribly superior to me. They write difficult verse."

It wasn't true, was it, that Mr. Forester (along with his gifted collaborators, John Huston and James Agee), was going to do a sequel to *The African Queen,* called "The African King"? No, it wasn't true. Was it all right to spike such a report? "Please do spike the rumor," Mr. Forester said with a show of enthusiasm. "I never *saw* the phrase, I never *heard* the phrase, until I read it in some newspaper reports."

It wasn't true, was it, that Mr. Forester had written *The African Queen* without ever having been to Africa? No, it wasn't true. "Though," he added, "I'd never been near the Rain Forest. I wrote *The Queen* in 1934. I remember it so well. One morning in London I saw my agent, who is still my friend. He told me a big London paper had got a new bee in its bonnet.

It was going to run serials from Monday through Friday, in five episodes."

Mr. Forester said epizodes. "Had I any ideas?" he continued. "They were paying good money. No, I don't have any. I got on the back car of my train and before I'd reached the head car the whole story started forming and was completely in my mind. I didn't bother to go home. If you've read the original script I daresay you may be able to detect the five climaxes. Later, I expanded it to the novel."

How did Mr. Forester live? Or, rather, *where* did he live? "In California. That's my home permanent. I lead a very nice life: June in England, October in New York and the rest in California, which I think—I really do—is the ideal life."

Had he found the movies a bad thing? "Oh no, no, no," Mr. Forester exclaimed. "When I was a young man it provided the money that set me free to do what I wanted."

A final question. What was an adventure novel? "I don't like analyzing myself," Mr. Forester said, "but recently I've come to an interesting conclusion. I rather fancy most authors think of a character and then think of what he would do. While I think of something to be done and then think of the most interesting character who could do it."

Perhaps that did define something?

"Yes," Mr. Forester said with positiveness, "I think it defines the adventure novel."

April 6, 1952

RALPH ELLISON

JUST over medium height and strong and substantial of physique, the author of *Invisible Man* is visible indeed. His face is firm and sensitive and remarkably handsome, a scar and a thin mustache failing to mar it. He's a standout in any company. The name is Ralph Ellison, heard here and there and one hopes everywhere these days because of his first, distinguished novel. And to be heard of in the future, if any predictions are worth anything at all.

Though up until this relatively triumphant event Mr. Ellison has been, it must be admitted, obscure. Before putting him on record as a thinking, talking chap, it seemed a good idea, therefore, to root around in Mr. Ellison's biography. It turned out he was born in Oklahoma City, in 1914. He lived there most of his life. Mr. Ellison spent three years at Tuskegee Institute, where he studied music and composition. Then he stumbled on sculpture.

That got him to New York, bent on exploring stone with a hammer and clay with a wire gimmick. Just about that time, though, along came *The Wasteland*—T. S. Eliot's, of course, and that turned out to be the most influential book in his life. "It got me interested in literature," Mr. Ellison said. "I tried to understand it better and that led me to reading criticism. I then started looking for Eliot's kind of sensibility in Negro poetry and I didn't find it until I ran into Richard Wright."

The work or the man? "Both," Mr. Ellison said. "We became friends, and still are. I began to write soon after. Meeting Wright at that time, when he hadn't yet begun to be famous, was most fortunate for me. He was passionately interested in the problems of technique and craft and it was an education. Later the Communists took credit for teaching him to write, but that's a lot of stuff. I published a short story in *American Writing*, I think, in 1940. I was in *Cross-Section*. That was, I believe, 1944, in which some of the first work of Norman Mailer, Arthur Miller and Shirley Jackson appeared."

Was *Invisible Man* Mr. Ellison's only novel? "I wrote a short novel in the process of writing this one," Mr. Ellison replied, "just to get a kindred theme out of the way."

Now, Mr. Ellison couldn't just slough off that one. How could he have been that clear? Why hadn't he been just enough confused—as most of us would be—to try to assimilate the kindred theme into the big novel? Mr. Ellison laughed a little. "I could see," he said, "it was not part of the novel because it had to do with a more mature character. While thematically it was part of the book, it nevertheless would have required different treatment; its reality wasn't as intense, as surreal, as the reality of the novel."

That was pretty much that then. Mr. Ellison continued. "Several reviews pointed out parts of the book they considered surrealistic. I'll agree with that; however I didn't select the surrealism, the distortion, the intensity, as an experimental technique but because reality is surreal. I used to get this same sense of a distorted reality years ago when I'd come every once in a while on a shell-shocked veteran of World War I. It was up in Harlem and he used to stop traffic on a street crossing by throwing imaginary bombs at the cars. Of course, the traffic flowed on quite normally. This fellow was reliving a trauma. But people were used to it and they went normally about their business."

What about the business (wasn't it nonsense?) of being a Negro writer? Wasn't one a writer who happened to be a Negro? Mr. Ellison tackled the question with what could only be called a beautiful honesty. "The thing that's forgotten is that everyone has to master his craft or profession. Without the mastery no one is free, Negro or white. You remember Hemingway saying he'd fought a draw with Balzac or whoever? Well, it's right. You enter into mortal combat with the best in your field. It at least keeps your feet on the ground," Mr. Ellison said laughingly. Hands clasped on the table, he went on:

"It is felt that there is something in the Negro experience that makes it not quite right for the novel. That's not true. It becomes important to the novelist because it is in this problem, as Faulkner makes us aware, that the American human conflict is at its most intense and dramatic. That's a rough way of putting it. What is exciting about it is that it hasn't really been written about except in a sociological way. That which for the sociologist presents itself as racial conflict becomes for the novelist the American form of the human drama. In Faulkner, Negro and white are catalyst for each other. If Faulkner could have found a more intense catalyst, he would have used it."

May 4, 1952

GEORGE JEAN NATHAN

FOR his seventieth birthday, George Jean Nathan received a splendid present: a sort of chrestomathy, a selection of his writings, titled *The World of George Jean Nathan*. Though no one was talking about Michelangelo, it seemed the right time to make our visit. Mr. Nathan, as every grown-up knows, is one of our nation's more distinguished and provocative gentlemen; and in his inimitably distinguished way, as editor, author and critic, has provoked considerable numbers of people over the years. Looking at Mr. Nathan, and listening, observing the gesture and heeding the speech, one is altogether struck by the fact that Mr. Nathan has style (as difficult to find these days as an honest man in Diogenes'); not stylishness, mind you, but style.

Still, even Mr. Nathan wasn't talking about Michelangelo. He was on birthday gifts, and he was particularly keen on a gift he got from one of the toy brothers Marx. "It's a radio," he said, with understated relish, "a radio," he then repeated with exaggerated awe, "that plays underwater." To accompany one while drowning? "Maybe to put out a call for help," Mr. Nathan said. Did it play above water? "That's another trouble," Mr. Nathan said quietly.

Mr. Nathan regarded a middle distance where presumably

247

the invisible radio sat. "It looks like a chromium bathtub," he said. "The porter stares at it with such love that I believe he'll soon own it. He wants to hear the baseball games. I haven't been much of a baseball fan. But did you ever eat the Stevens Brothers' frankfurters at the Yankee Stadium clubhouse? They are probably the best thing about baseball. Winston Churchill eats twenty-two of them at a time, without mustard. I can eat twenty of them."

With or without mustard, Mr. Nathan must have a pretty good view of the cultural scene stretching back quite a way. Would he consider a summation? Mr. Nathan nodded briefly.

"In drama," he said, "the emergence of O'Neill. In criticism, before O'Neill, James Huneker [Mr. Nathan didn't say Hew-nuh-kuh, or Hew-nee-ker, but, and apparently properly, Hun-uh-kuh]. In literature I would give not the conventional answer of the Twenties and such; rather it was the emergence of—it's obvious, rather obvious—the Dreisers, Lewises and Cabells. That, in looking over the panorama of my own time, seems sound criticism."

Mr. Nathan gestured. "We're just speaking of the seeds and to some extent the blossoms," he warned. "Huneker," Mr. Nathan said, "freed, brought in a sweep. It was Huneker, it was he who put a brilliant tie around what were the choke collars of American criticism. O'Neill was the first man who set himself the problem of writing serious American drama, who brought to it a depth, a psychological depth, a courage for tragedy, for honest tragedy (there was tragedy before, but it was bogus). He was honest about men and women."

Mr. Nathan paused, gazing about the room neutrally. "In literature there were men before the men I mentioned," Mr. Nathan said, "men like Howells, but there wasn't the experience, the depth to achieve the experience. I'd say these men achieved something significant: Dreiser seriously, Cabell humorously and satirically, Lewis reportorially and instinctively. This is the seed and the seed did produce its blossoms and perhaps the finest blossom was the emergence of Hemingway. There was also the endless influence he has had on inferior men. If there had never been, as we know, a war or a series of wars there would still have been a Hemingway. But what about his imitators? And his detractors? Their incompetence has been proven."

It was difficult to resist—considering Mr. Nathan's calm worldliness—a timely question: what about this Presidential year? "Oh," Mr. Nathan said politely yet disdainfully, "I take no interest in politics. A man who takes an interest in politics plays around with that little quicksilver toy he played with as a child. It is the diversion of trivial men and when they succeed at it they become important in the eyes of more trivial men."

Could Mr. Nathan say that Roosevelt was trivial, or Eisenhower? "I don't think Eisenhower is interested in politics," Mr. Nathan replied. "A man who is interested in being President isn't necessarily interested in politics."

What then would such a man be interested in? "There's a constant search for honors, and I think it's understandable. Who," Mr. Nathan asked, perhaps deliberately, "is the other man you spoke of?" It was Roosevelt. "Which one?" he asked. Oh, either—Franklin D. or Teddy. "Let's not speak disrespectfully of the dead," Mr. Nathan said, as he sipped his drink and stared owlishly over his highball glass.

May 11, 1952

CARL SANDBURG

CARL SANDBURG seems a tall man though he isn't; and approaching seventy-five, he seems a young man. He is a bony, fine-looking fellow, with flattened-down, white, symmetrical hair (that can get quite disheveled), enigmatic eyes, a bold nose and mouth. He is master of a considerable number of significant activities, and he wins all the prizes. Poet, novelist, historian, biographer, humorist, journalist, balladeer, goat-farmer, he has just received the Gold Medal for History and Biography from the National Institute and American Academy of Arts and Letters, because of his monumental six-volume Lincoln biography, *The Prairie Years* and *The War Years* (1926-1939).

Obviously, he has come a long way since the early days when he was a milk-wagon driver in Illinois, a wheat harvester in Kansas, a dish washer in Colorado, a coal shoveler in Omaha and a soldier in Puerto Rico during the Spanish-American War. Come a long way—but not changed so you could notice it. When you say, "What will you do with your Gold Medal?" he laughs uninhibitedly, and answers: "I'll wear it on the inside of my coat and when a railroad dick stops me and flashes his badge, I'll flash my gold badge right back at him." Not changed at all. Sometimes you may see him slicked up in blue serge and fresh white shirt, but he'll also be wearing his old tan, cracked

251

work shoes—maybe for comfort, maybe for a symbol even, a reminder of the old times.

Carl Sandburg is a freewheeling free man—an improviser, a spontaneous, unfettered monologist. Around him, dialogue barely exists, and when it does he molds it into unorthodoxy, answering with sly, wise, oblique phrases in a tough, mellifluent bass that ranges the scales as dramatically as did the great Chaliapin's in a recitative. Imagine then, the Sandburg voice, at one moment as soft as the wind among the reeds, at another as explosive as thunder in a bowling alley, and with all the modulations between, on a variety of topics, including the following:

Childhood: By a process of deduction, when I arrived as a newborn child I undoubtedly had diapers made of Pillsbury sacks. I am sure it was a cornhusk mattress I was born on because until I was twelve or fourteen there were cornhusk mattresses for all my family.

Movies, Radio, TV: I am disgusted. The habit grows of sitting up to them, sitting up to those machines, listening and looking for hours on hours on hours. There are good things to see and hear in them, priceless things, but for those who are not on the watch, these machines are thieves of time, with not even a mechanical conscience about the hours and hours they will waste in a day.

People: Long before these new educational mechanisms, these devices in the field of culture, there were men with sublime personalities, deep-rooted, that we love to contemplate. Not one of them ever saw a movie or heard a radio or watched a TV. Lincoln, Robert E. Lee, Jefferson, Leonardo, Shakespeare and many others, some of them hundreds of years ago. There were no signs of these modern mechanisms; but out of books and solitude they sank deep roots and effloresced.

Character: Personality is the key. The men of grand personality were not afraid of loneliness. Every sublime creative artist and inventor has valued loneliness. Some philosopher long ago wrote it down that there were persons to whom nothing was more difficult than to sit in a quiet room alone. I will tell you of an interview that once ran in *The New York Times*, an interview with an important television script writer getting a thousand dollars a week. He went into methods of writing, of what the public likes, and then away down at the bottom of the column came the question from the very intelligent reporter: Do you have a television set in your home? And the answer: No, we want our children to read books.

Politics: Huey Long was a far more creative, more imaginative man, with far more color, than Joe McCarthy.

Poetry: Does it have a future? Bobby Burns is going to go along and he'll be traveling when several figures of higher acclaim have just vanished beyond the green horizons. Robert Frost is a fine poet most of the time. His work is read by strong men, farmers, thieves and deacons—and not by little cliques.

Newspapers: I read the papers a lot. I go with Robert Louis Stevenson who said that an intelligent reader with imagination can make an Iliad of a newspaper.

Work in Progress: Yes, I am writing a memory book. Yes, but it ain't an autobiography, it ain't no autobiography. It's memories—of persons, places and things I've been a part of. There I go ending up in a preposition again.

June 1, 1952

JAMES THURBER

‾‾

THIS column, in order that it get written, requires (in the language of the fourth estate) a news peg. Once a week, presumably, an author is in the news: he has written a book, or he has come back from a long journey, or he has a novel opinion about civil liberties or a civil opinion about novels. For this column's safety-deposit holdings, though, no news peg is required to have a talk, even a formal talk, with James Grover Thurber. As luck would have it, however, there turned out to be three news pegs to justify (where no justification was required) a talk with Jim Thurber. Mr. Thurber has a new book out, *The Thurber Album* (it has made the best-seller chart); Mr. Thurber, together with collaborator Elliott Nugent, has *The Male Animal* once again tickling the collective ribs of the playgoing mobs; and Mr. Thurber has returned to America after one hundred days of absence.

On the 101st day, that is on the first day back, Mr. and Mrs. Thurber had lunch at their usual midtown hotel. One by one the men who help make *The New Yorker* a brilliant magazine came by and greeted Mr. Thurber, remarked on his stay, congratulated him on his play and on his book. Then the various maîtres came over and welcomed him. Finally the waiters who weren't waiting on his table came over and saluted him. It was

255

a tribute that Mr. Thurber took head bowed, as it were, and muttering with pleasure and embarrassment into the table. The fifty-seven-year-old Mr. Thurber, as a matter of fact, looks well —though he has lost some weight which he can ill afford to lose. His face was healthily burned and he looked rested. "I ought to look rested," Mr. Thurber said, "I didn't do a damn thing."

Being an old hand at reporting, Mr. Thurber decided to help along. "About the book," he began, "you can say it's about Taft country but it's by an Eisenhower man." Mr. Thurber, thinking on politics and the state of the Union, took a jump or two. "If we don't stop suspecting all writers," he said, "it will be a severe blow to our culture. I think all writers, even the innocent ones, are scared. There's guilt by association, guilt by excoriation, there's guilt by everything the politicians invent. And it's rather foolish to hold the respect we do for ex-Communists, that is, people who once tried to overthrow the Government. Pretty soon some new Budenz will drop out of The Party deliberately, and we will go ahead and make him a hero."

Just about that time Elliott Nugent visited briefly, and when he left, Mr. Thurber picked up the thread of the discussion. "People ask why there isn't a comedy like *The Male Animal* any more—something that's free and exuberant. It isn't possible to write a comedy like that any more because we're living in the most frightened country in the world. How confusing my dossier must be. I wouldn't join a Communist organization, obviously. But I won't be scared off those organizations I did sign up for. They say now—it's gotten so abject—don't join anything. Don't even join a garden club."

None of it was funny; Mr. Thurber wasn't feeling funny. Still, Mr. Thurber ought to talk about humor, oughtn't he? "Humor isn't considered one of the major arts," Mr. Thurber said, after the briefest pause. "The best essay on humor I know was written by Andy White in *A Subtreasury of American*

Humor. I guess books of humor don't last because, like the passions, humor is a changing thing. It is likely to date because it deals in the modern idiom. I wonder about *Babbitt*, whether the humor in that wouldn't date? According to Mencken," Mr. Thurber said, "there are only two American novels, *Babbitt* and *Huck Finn*. The best estimate of my work was done by T. S. Eliot."

Mr. Thurber shook his head affirmatively. "Most humorous books date and the serious books don't," he said. "When you see *As You Like It* you know it was written over 250 years ago." What about a book like *Tristram Shandy?* "I haven't tried those old books. I can't get through *Pickwick Papers*. And don't forget, there's a cult around the old work which makes it difficult to know when it's funny and when it's supposed to be funny. I can't remember any humor in old Scott Fitzgerald. Humor would have saved him. It seems to me the great novelists have humor in them, even if it isn't predominant. The Russians had it; Gogol had it, and Dostoevsky. It seems to me Fitzgerald strangled humor because he was caught in the romantic tradition. Well, there isn't a trace of humor in communism, is there? I think any political system that vehemently attacks humor reveals a great weakness. It is one of the dangers universally. One of the great things we have here is humor—even in war. We ought not to lose that."

June 29, 1952

FRANK O'CONNOR

LAST year—on June 24, 1951, to be precise—this column carried a "talk" with the Irish writer, Frank O'Connor. Only, to be precise for the second and last time, it wasn't a "talk." Mr. O'Connor had written a letter, answers to questions asked him, and these answers became the talk. Only they weren't so much answers as improvisations—and these were characterized by wit, intelligence, honesty and spirit. Well, Mr. O'Connor has been around the States a bit now, and he has been met, and it is nice to be able to report that the gent in the flesh is not a particle less witty or intelligent or honest or spirited (or handsome) than the letter-writer.

It was Nietzsche who said that the mind must learn to think as a form of dancing; it is Mr. O'Connor's mind that exemplifies what the philosopher had in mind. So let us put an end to this transient impression of Mr. O'Connor, and let us begin. "I began very early," Mr. O'Connor said about his profession. "I started producing my first collected editions at the age of twelve. I was intended by God to be a painter. But I was very poor, and pencil and paper were the cheapest. Music was out for that reason as well. Literature is the poor man's art," Mr. O'Connor concluded with a gnomic flourish.

Now, that first collection, that prodigy of labor, what was in it? "The pieces consisted of poems and biographies and essays on history, particularly on the grievances [pronounced in a subtle, musical cross between greevences and grayvances] of Ireland. The first things I published," Mr. O'Connor continued, less jocularly, "were two translations of Du Bellay—from a language I didn't know (French) into a language I didn't know (Irish). At least, I didn't know the latter in any grammatical way; my grandmother spoke Irish."

But now Mr. O'Connor knew Irish? "Oh, yes," he said, "I really settled down to learn it in a proper way. All my early work and my friend Seán O'Faoláin's were written in Irish."

There was a charming book Mr. O'Connor had written, *Towards an Appreciation of Literature*, and in it the reader discovered that the writer, one-time librarian in Cork County and Dublin, was completely self-taught. Mr. O'Connor shook his head, both affirming and denying. "There was one man who did influence me; it was Daniel Corkery, a remarkable man. This little, limping teacher, with a little, black mustache, wrote something on the blackboard I had never seen before: 'Awaken your courage, Ireland.' It was an admonition to himself, too. After that he published a book of short stories and a novel. The novel, *The Threshold of Quiet*, was brilliant. Corkery, you see, was the first Irishman to introduce the Russian note into literature—and that's the thing O'Faoláin and I have built on."

The author waved away a cloud of cigarette smoke. "The trouble with our two big men, Yeats and Joyce"—Mr. O'Connor gestured in supplementary explanation—"idealism and naturalism. After the Civil War both were useless."

In reply to the mute question, Mr. O'Connor proceeded. "We needed a realism which would unite the idealism of Yeats with the naturalism, the truthfulness of Joyce. It's really a form of poetic realism, nothing more, that we needed. Sean O'Casey is the last of the idealistic thesis. It wasn't possible after the blood and crash of the Civil War. O'Casey crashed it down. In Joyce there was a growing disillusion with materialism, which ended up in the sort of logical chaos of *Finnegans Wake*."

Would Mr. O'Connor take Joyce's lovely stories, *The Dubliners*? He would. Wouldn't he agree that in them one found poetic realism? "Yes," Mr. O'Connor said, "yes. It would be fair to say that in the beginning Joyce did have it. 'The Dead' is an amazing construct. But we've never given a damn about form."

Yet Mr. O'Connor himself had form! "Ah, yes! But it's the form of life itself," Mr. O'Connor countered. "It's not imposed form. I want form to follow a man's life or a man's character. The form is inherent in the experience. I get exactly the same feeling from a Ben Jonson play as I get from Joyce's novel. The Shakespearean stuff had the organic form as opposed to the imposed form of Jonson. Chekhov is wonderful for that: the completely organic form. I think fundamentally it goes back to a man's attitude to life. In Chekhov you feel that life is dictating to him; in Joyce he is dictating to life. I'm not saying for an instant that the writer is passive to life. He is *giving* himself to it. He just says to life, 'Oh, *that's* what you mean? That's grand! Carry on.' "

August 24, 1952

ERNEST HEMINGWAY

THIS week Mr. Ernest Hemingway is the news truly. Not only the literary news. Like Earl Sande booting home a Derby winner, or Johnny Vander Meer pitching two no-hitters in succession, or the Manassa Mauler battering big Jess Willard, a book by Papa is front-page news. This fact creates certain misunderstandings. Mr. Hemingway seems to be in the news more than he actually is only because each time he makes his move it starts talk. This is not his fault, and the people who think of Mr. Hemingway as a chap who likes moving into the spotlight are not less than dead wrong. As a matter of record, it would be difficult to find a writer who lives more privately, minding his own business and cultivating his own garden (in the best Voltairean sense of the phrase).

Well, here we are too, just as meddlesome as the rest. Mr. Hemingway writes a small, fine novel, *The Old Man and the Sea*, and instead of letting him be, and being happy about it, we're after him—and there is no discharge from the war. True, we went after him equivocally, ridden by a guilt sufficient to prevent us from asking questions. We merely asked him for a statement, or a number of statements, on whatever was occupying him at the time. Pro and gallant that he is, Mr. Hemingway kicked through with a set of answers to a set of questions that he himself devised. Without further ado, then, here is Mr. Hemingway answering Mr. Hemingway:

Q. How do you feel, Mr. H.?

A. Very well, thank you.

Q. What are your plans?

A. To take a vacation, if I have any money left after taxes, and then go back to work.

Q. Where would you like to take your vacation?

A. Either out West or in Europe.

Q. Do you enjoy writing, Mr. H.?

A. Very much. But if you do it as well as you can each day, it is tiring.

Q. Do you mind talking about it?

A. I do not believe in talking about it and I try to avoid talking about it. If I have to talk about a book that I have written it destroys the pleasure I have from writing it. If the writing is any good everything there is to say has been conveyed to the reader.

Q. What about fishing?

A. I have enjoyed it ever since I can remember. But I do not enjoy talking about it except to professional fishermen. One of the reasons I quit fishing at Bimini was to avoid the nightly post mortems of the anglers. Another was because the big fish caught were wasted. No fish caught in Cuba is wasted.

Q. Do you spend much time on the sea?

A. In twenty years of my life probably half of it has been spent on the sea.

Q. Can you work while at sea?

A. Perhaps better than anywhere else. My boat, The Pilar,* has no radio, no telephone and, since the war, no radio communications of any kind. You can anchor in the lee of some bay in

* The name of the blasphemous and noblehearted matriarch of *For Whom the Bell Tolls*.

the Gulf Stream and write on a writing board with no intrusions and you have no excuses if you fail to work well.

Q. Does your wife like the sea?

A. She loves it very much. She has never been seasick and she loves to swim and fish, all kinds of fishing, and to watch the stars at night.

Q. Do you have a happy life, Mr. Hemingway?

A. I have never heard a happy life defined. I have always been happy when I am working. If I cannot work I usually do something bad and have remorse and then my conscience makes me work. A conscience tells truths that are as uncomfortable as those a compass sometimes shows. Personally I am happy when I work hard and love someone. Since I have done both these things now for a long time I would say I have a happy life. Times have always been bad. But Walter Raleigh wrote very well the night before he climbed the steps to the scaffold erected in the Old Palace yard of Westminster. I see no reason now not to write well because the times are bad both for those who write and those who read.

September 7, 1952

EDMUND WILSON

~·~

THE naked facts, the vital statistics, on Edmund Wilson, author of the just published *Shores of Light,* do not tell the story. Mr. Wilson was born in Red Bank, New Jersey, in 1895; is Princeton, class of '16; worked as a reporter on the old *New York Evening Sun,* was managing editor of *Vanity Fair,* an associate editor of *The New Republic,* and book columnist for *The New Yorker,* and is of course the author of a considerable number of distinguished books. What it adds up to is a lifetime of serious writing. What it doesn't signify is the quality of Mr. Wilson's labors. And it ought to be said at once, as one man's opinion, unqualified: Mr. Wilson is really America's number one man of letters. What does that mean, you ask? It means that Mr. Wilson brings to his critical pursuits more relevant weapons (or more appropriate loves) than any other critic writing today, and is consequently best equipped to disclose the defects and virtues in a work of art.

This is a good deal. Mr. Wilson, medium height, with a hard plumpness to him, and whose face is stunningly classic in profile (all in all looking a good deal like a top-level Roman Senator), doesn't deny it. Not that he would draw the conclusions drawn above; Mr. Wilson isn't modest, but neither is he immodest. What he is is matter-of-fact about himself, stating what he knows and doesn't know as though he were somebody else.

"My function, such as it is," Mr. Wilson said in dealing with Mr. Wilson as a critic, "nobody ever brings out. I'll tell you what I think it is. My function is to bring together a number of fields that haven't been brought together. I'm not saying I'm an authority in any of them. I read a great deal of English literature. I have read a lot of French and Italian literature, and I got seriously interested in American literature, which I'm reading in more and more."

Mr. Wilson got off the arm of the chair he was sitting on and took a short stroll about the room. "So that I knew something about English literature and Continental writing and the American writer," he summed up. "And then I got interested in Marxism," he said. "I went to Russia and studied the language. I did know these different kinds of things and tried to bring them together. I think what I have tried to do was to get a point of view into literary life which was not provincial. You know, George Saintsbury tried to produce something that was very worthy, a history of the literature of the whole world. The work is strangely provincial even though Saintsbury was probably the English critic with the broadest point of view."

Mr. Wilson's eyes were bright as brown diamonds. "I'm not learned in any of the fields," he reiterated. "I'm merely trying to correlate many things. What I don't know anything about is Spanish and Latin American literature because I don't like reading translations." Mr. Wilson took a little walk. "Some day," he said, coming back to within hearing range of his visitor, "I'll learn Spanish."

He sat down, thought a moment. "The aim," he said, "is to be truly international. My idea is that an American can do this. The English and French are provincial. The Russians are marvelously intelligent and well-read, but their intellectual development has been arrested by the turn their communism has taken.

Aside from Russians and Americans, the Roman intellectual is the most international. But there is a cynicism there, too, unattached to any cultural movement and it is a little defeating."

In the light, or darkness of all that, did Mr. Wilson know what he would be doing next? Mr. Wilson said he did. "I'm engaged on a book that will take in the literature in America between the years 1870 to 1910. My idea is that the earlier period has been pretty well excavated. It won't be comprehensive. It will deal with more or less selected subjects. It is a neglected period. Van Wyck Brooks' last volume is the only book that deals with it. The American literary histories that deal with it are completely inadequate. Some of the most important people are not mentioned at all, or are hardly mentioned, and Brooks is the only writer who has read that period and knows it."

Mr. Wilson stopped and started again with abruptness. "I read *Tristram Shandy* when I was about fifteen and I also read Taine's reference to Sterne in which he used the metaphor of the magnifying glass. That was really the thing that started me off, my first literary stirrings. I did a paper on Sterne for my English master. What I produced was not a critical essay but a fictional study of Sterne, a psychological study." Mr. Wilson laughed a little at how it had turned out. "My first critical effort," he said, "turned out to be a psychological study in fictional form. It really defied classification. My work still is hard to classify, isn't it?"

November 2, 1952

SAUL BELLOW

IT WAS of Dostoevsky that André Gide once said all factions could find something in him to support their claims but no one faction could claim him exclusively. Some of this holds true for Saul Bellow. He came up as a writer out of the tough, tight literary magazines, established his beachhead, as it were, and is now successfully fanning out into the broader and brighter domains; his talents, valued from the start by the severer literary critics, have gradually begun to be noticed by greater numbers of the ordinary, intelligent vintage. Mr. Bellow's work contains innumerably diverse elements, it has variousness and is against the grain. His readers, therefore, are to be found anywhere and everywhere and they can be anyone at all.

Mr. Bellow's face has variousness, too: sharply etched, the structure conveys scientific coldness; but the texture is bold, lyric, poetic. And similarly with his manner: he will talk on the most abstruse or delicate or complex subjects in a matter-of-fact, even breezy, colloquial. What he renders unto Caesar is public, what he renders unto God is a strictly private matter.

His first leap into the swaddling-banded world was in 1915, in Quebec. His father, living in Petrograd, had been importing Egyptian onions. He decided to migrate to Canada because his sister was living there. In telling it, Mr. Bellow said in an aside that his father was a fascinating character. Since *The Adventures of Augie March* was a big novel, one wondered whether his father was in it? "No," Mr. Bellow said laughingly, "I've saved him."

From Canada to Chicago, at the age of nine, and there the youthful Bellow remained for quite a while. Two years at the University of Chicago, brought him around to the conclusion that the study of literature was not the best way to become a writer. He decided to become an anthropologist and he buried himself in the stacks of Northwestern University, working under the famed Professor Herskovits (who wanted to make a pianist out of him). He next got a scholarship at Wisconsin, where he plugged at his master's thesis in anthropology. There Dr. Goldenweiser assured him he wasn't cut out for science. His papers had too much style. "It was a nice way of easing me out of the field," Mr. Bellow said.

"Goldenweiser played Chopin and wept. He was very Chekhovian. The old boy's heart was really in literature. Every time I worked on my thesis, it turned out to be a story. I disappeared for the Christmas holidays and I never came back." Mr. Bellow laughed a little, and then said, "This is my way of making a change. Disappearing from something and never coming back."

And so at this juncture began "The Adventures of Saul Bellow" because at this point he started to write. Between then and *Augie March*, Mr. Bellow had written two novels, *Dangling Man* and *The Victim*. Mr. Bellow nodded, but contradicted. "This is the third published novel. I threw two novels away because they were too sad."

Mr. Bellow has written steadily all the while—short stories, essays, literary articles. He won a Guggenheim Fellowship and a National Institute of Arts and Letters Award. Along the way he taught at the University of Minnesota and at Princeton. He

has taken a job on the English staff of Bard College—which
brings our author up to the immediate present. Except for
Augie. Would Mr. Bellow tell us what he could?

He thought a bit and then said, "I started *Augie* in Paris. I
wrote it in trains and cafés. I got used to writing on the roll. I
hunted for the right café in Rome, and, when I found it, I
worked there all the time. After I was there about a month, the
waiter told me it was where D'Annunzio used to come to write.
But," Mr. Bellow added dryly, "I don't expect to get into
politics."

Had he had any trouble getting so right a name as Augie
March? Mr. Bellow shook his head negatively, almost sleepily.
"It just came to me," he said. "The great pleasure of the book
was that it came easily. All I had to do was be there with buckets
to catch it. That's why the form is loose."

Then it had just flowed easily and loosely and there was no
literary principle back of the looseness? "Something like that,"
Mr. Bellow replied. "But I do think that the novel has imitated
poetry far too much recently." How had it done that? "In its
severity and style and devotion to exact form. In the great period
of the novel, the novelist didn't care—there was a great mass of
sand and gravel; there was diversity of scene, a large number of
characters. One of the reasons the novel has diminished is that
a great many people, writers, find it difficult to write dramatic
scenes.

"After all, the novel grew out of daily events, out of newspapers. Today, the novelist thinks too much of immortality and
he tries to create form. He tries to make his work durable
through form. But you have to take your chances on mortality,
on perishability. That's what I felt. I kicked over the traces,
wrote catch-as-catch-can, picaresque. I took my chance."

Mr. Bellow shrugged, smiled and made his momentous novel

seem casual. It was, we were convinced, what he wanted and needed to do. Obviously, Mr. Bellow was against the over-solemn, the too-pious manner, the inflated ego. Who could be against Mr. Bellow for that?

September 20, 1953

ERNEST HEMINGWAY

～

IN HAVANA, on October 28, the weather was calm and pleasant. No threat of hurricanes on that day, but plenty of people milling around Finca Vigia, Ernest Hemingway's home outside the capital of Cuba. Two hours before talking to him on the telephone, the news had come officially from Stockholm that Hemingway had won the Nobel Prize. Days before, the rumors had begun and the press was alerted and present.

Now he was on the phone. Over it came noise: agitated sea voices. He sounded neither enthusiastic nor indifferent. He sounded in dead control, and his voice was slow and distinct and careful. There were shouts and low-voiced conversations, coming apparently from behind his back. But he was patient, and his attitude was "go ahead and shoot." He was ready to talk.

About writing Hemingway said: "What a writer must try to do is to write as truly as he can. For a writer of fiction has to invent out of what he knows in order to make something not photographic, or naturalistic, or realistic, which will be something entirely new and invented out of his own knowledge.

"What a writer should try to do is to make something which will be so written that it will become a part of the experience of those who read him."

And criticism: "I have learned very much from criticism—when it was of a simple nature. When criticism described me as arrogant, proud or attributed to me other venial sins, I did not learn. I believe that critics know very little about the alchemy of the production of literature. I believe the microphone is one of the greatest enemies of literature, of letters, and that a man should try to imply or show in his written words what he believes, rather than put it into speeches or discourses."

He was reminded that the Italian writer Ignazio Silone once had been asked what was the most important date in history, and that Silone had answered, "the twenty-fifth of December, Year Zero." Hemingway replied, "I have no important dates. And I have never believed in astrology nor in any of the occult sciences. I do not know what Man (with a capital M) means. I do know what a man (small m) is. I do know what man (with a small m) means and I hope I have learned something about men (small m) and something about women and something about animals."

What was he working on now?

With patience and exactness, Hemingway said, "I started to write three short stories about Africa for the collection of stories that Charles Scribner's are planning to publish. There are some seven unpublished stories. I wrote the first story and then when I was well into the second, it started to be a novel. I am writing on this story now—I am writing on this now and it is, as always, both bad and difficult to discuss what you are writing."

And finally: "As a Nobel Prize winner I cannot but regret that the award was never given to Mark Twain, nor to Henry James, speaking only of my own countrymen. Greater writers than these also did not receive the prize.

"I would have been happy—happier—today if the prize had gone to that beautiful writer Isak Dinesen, or to Bernard Berenson, who has devoted a lifetime to the most lucid and best writ-

ERNEST HEMINGWAY 277

ing on painting that has been produced, and I would have been most happy to know that the prize had been awarded to Carl Sandburg.

"Since I am not in a position to—no—since I respect and honor the decision of the Swedish Academy, I should not make any such observation. Anyone receiving an honor must receive it in humility."

Though Hemingway is only fifty-five, the prize—highest in value and most distinguished in honor—has been a long time coming. From the beginning, in 1924, when Hemingway published a collection of stories called *In Our Time*, it was apparent that a remarkable and an original talent had entered our life and letters. Any question as to his formidable gifts and art and discipline became idle when, two years later, Hemingway published his first big novel, *The Sun Also Rises*.

He became the most influential and most imitated writer. He dared deal (without saying so in speech or discourse) with what Faulkner has called "the eternal verities of the heart." Passion and wit, brutality and love, lust and ethical concern, action and morality all found their substantial shapes in Hemingway's terse, quintessential and yet (paradoxically) natural language.

What he wrote did become a part of the experience of those who read him. What Hemingway has attempted throughout his career (throughout his life) was no esthetic end so much as a metaphysical one: every clear, strong, crisp word seemed to give expression to the basic attitudes he has held toward all life— so that what one received from him was not a fragment of art so much as the totality of his being. It was concealed, of course, by the best and most natural craftsman of our time. But it was there. One experienced a man engaged with all his seriousness in the serious business of discovering the secrets of life and living. One got it from Balzac in that way, too; in a more intellectual way from Stendhal; and in a more oblique way from Henry James.

A serious writer is, after all, a medium. He himself is the medium. Everything that happens to such a writer, everything that is usable that he experiences—sees, smells, hears, notes—finds its true shape through that medium. So that it could be imagined that what "happened" to Chekhov became short stories at the instant they entered Chekhov's life; or to Yeats, poems; or to Gide, exquisite entries into journals (that is, essentially shapeless).

What results if the serious writer is an artist is a work of real power, because the work is relentlessly honest and relentlessly and intransigently the expression of one's own self. Hemingway's art has had this impact of life, but without the verbiage of art or the muddle of life. It was true from the beginning.

Why then did the "official" recognition come so belatedly? Aside from factors that one can only guess at, each generation takes what it needs, or thinks it wants—and to my mind a crucial job of criticism is precisely to discern what each generation needs. One read *The Sun Also Rises*, and took from it the running of the bulls, the fight between boxer and torero, the cruelty of Brett. One took from *Death in the Afternoon* the eulogy of violence.

What has happened now is that we are reading Hemingway with greater balance, discovering freshly the beauty of the pastoral in those fishing scenes of *The Sun Also Rises*, the brief and charming relations between American and Spaniard, the moral concern of Brett. In *Death in the Afternoon* one finds the eulogy of valor. Certain events, foreground for another generation, recede for ours, and backgrounds come forward. The humanity and compassion and humility are now established in Hemingway's world as much as conflict and death and violence were for another.

Such readings in the text have obviously seeped down (or up) to the authorities who make momentous decisions. This "time-lag" is not necessarily regrettable, though terrible oversights are made during one's lifetime. Joyce did not get a Nobel Prize; Yeats did.

Happily, Hemingway has lived a long time in his short life and he has survived much, including the factions, the critics and the officials. He has lived long enough to see many changes. Year after year, when the prize was awarded to lesser writers, or to less influential writers, Hemingway never complained. He was always gracious. He does not complain now, either.

November 7, 1954

WILLIAM FAULKNER

WE STARTED out on a walk, and William Faulkner said, "I find Park Avenue is the best street to walk on" (though it sounded closer to "Ah fahnd Pahk Avenoo"). We headed toward it in the twilight. He was a small, slight figure, contained and unhurried, in the madding crowd that pressed anarchically ahead for Grand Central and its neighboring subway stations. He wore his Dragnet trenchcoat, an Alpine hat, and he held his pipe in a gloved hand. He looked into a variety of shop windows for long impassive moments. To me it was a foregone conclusion that he would say nothing revelatory about his recent novel, *A Fable*, which had just been honored by the National Book Award as the best fiction for 1954. Nevertheless, I asked him.

"There is nothing to say about it," Mr. Faulkner said in his unbelievably musical voice and speech. "I did the best I could, and if there's something more I could say, I'd have said it in the book. There's nothing I could add to it. I think if I would do it over, maybe I would do it better, but I always think that with everything I've done, as any artist thinks. The work never matches the dream of perfection the artist had to start with."

Suddenly Mr. Faulkner's mood changed: he grew excited. It was a small change, not greatly disparate from his earlier impassivity, but the change was apparent and dramatic, just as the modulated shift in mood in a piece of chamber music can be more dramatic than a big change in a symphony. "That's what I had in mind when I talked about Hemingway being a coward. I was quoted out of context. I had in mind this dream of perfection and how the best contemporary writers failed to match it. I was asked the question down at the University of Mississippi——"

Hold on, I thought, hold on, Mr. Faulkner. Let's take it from the beginning. "Let's go over the whole thing," Mr. Faulkner said, and I knew then that this was one of those Faulkner days when I didn't need to say anything to him. "I was asked the question who were the five best contemporary writers and how did I rate them. And I said Wolfe, Hemingway, Dos Passos, Caldwell and myself. I rated Wolfe first, myself second. I put Hemingway last. I said we were all failures. All of us had failed to match the dream of perfection and I rated the authors on the basis of their splendid failure to do the impossible. I believed Wolfe tried to do the greatest of the impossible, that he tried to reduce all human experience to literature. And I thought after Wolfe I had tried the most. I rated Hemingway last because he stayed within what he knew. He did it fine, but he didn't try for the impossible."

We were walking along Park Avenue toward the Grand Central Arcade. "I hate to think that Grand Central's coming down," he said. I remembered that Faulkner long ago had written a sleepy story about Grand Central Station. He nodded, recollecting the story. "I rated those authors by the way in which they failed to match the dream of perfection," he said. "This had nothing to do with the value of the work, the impact or perfection of its own kind that it had. I was talking only about the magnificence of the failure, the attempt to do the impossible within human experience."

It followed, then, that from other points of view the five

artists could be rated differently? Mr. Faulkner nodded in agreement and the particular discussion was dropped. We waited for
a traffic light, and he listened with his own kind of stillness
that, more powerful than the noise around us, subdued it. What
were his plans? Was he going off again, or staying on, or what?

"I might be going to Europe this spring—for the State Department," he told me. "It's a possibility." He and Robert
Frost had gone to South America not so long ago—that was a
good sign. "The writer in America isn't part of the culture of
this country. He's like a fine dog. People like him around, but
he's of no use."

Perhaps because of the cold war and the Soviet emphasis on
culture, our country was growing up to the realization that its
artists could make a strong contribution?

Mr. Faulkner wasn't sure. "Unless," he said, "someone somewhere had enough sense to go to someone in a high position and
said, 'Let's see Robert Frost instead of Henry Ford for a change.'
Or someone here said to someone there, 'What can we do for
you to show you a side of our country you don't know?'

"The artist is still a little like the old court jester. He's supposed to speak his vicious paradoxes with some sense in them,
but he isn't part of whatever the fabric is that makes a nation.
It is assumed that anyone who makes a million dollars has a
unique gift, though he might have made it off some useless
gadget."

We talked more, and I told Mr. Faulkner that I thought of
his short novel, *The Bear*, as a modern *Moby Dick*. Mr. Faulkner, rejecting the "provocation," said, "Now that's odd. The
new book we're getting together starts off with that story." The
book, we learned, will be out this year. "It's a collection of my
hunting stories, and we're calling it 'Big Woods.' I have written some remarks before each of the stories——"

Sort of commentaries? I asked. "Well," Mr. Faulkner said,

shaking his head. "I think that's a bad word. I'd call them interrupted catalysts."

We came up to Grand Central and we shook hands. I told him to take care of himself. He smiled, and asked, "What're you going to do now?" I told him I thought I'd find a barber and get a shave. He said, "That's a good idea. There ought to be a good barber right here in Grand Central."

January 30, 1955

INDEX OF AUTHORS INTERVIEWED

About the Author

HARVEY BREIT, assistant editor of *The New York Times Book Review*, was born in New York City in 1913. He never finished his schooling and owns no degrees. In New Mexico in the middle 1930's he began to write in earnest, and for the next five years he devoted himself mainly to verse, an activity that resulted in a book of poems, *There Falls Tom Fool*. In the middle 1940's Mr. Breit went to work for *The New York Times* Sunday Department, first in its magazine section, subsequently in its book section. At the present time he writes a weekly column, "In and Out of Books."

Mr. Breit has written introductions to a reprint edition of William Faulkner's *Absalom, Absalom!* and to J. F. Byrne's *Silent Years, an Autobiography with Memoirs of James Joyce and Our Ireland*. In 1952 he took a six-month leave of absence from *The Times* to go to India for the Ford Foundation, where he edited a contemporary collection of Indian writing, *Perspectives of India*. He is married to Patricia Rinehart, and lives in New York City.

Wilmington Public Library
Wilmington, N. C.